KENNETH D. KING'S
Smart Fitting
SOLUTIONS

Foolproof Techniques to Fit Any Figure

- READ THE WRINKLES
- DECIPHER THE MESSAGE
- FIX THE FIT

The Taunton Press

Text © 2018 Kenneth D. King
Photographs © 2018 by The Taunton Press, Inc.
Illustrations © 2018 by The Taunton Press, Inc.

 **The Taunton Press**
Inspiration for hands-on living®

The Taunton Press, Inc.
63 South Main Street
PO Box 5506
Newtown, CT 06470-5506
Email: tp@taunton.com

Editor: Judith Neukam
Copy Editor: Betty Christiansen
Indexer: Jim Curtis
Art Director: Rosalind Loeb
Jacket/Cover design: Kim Adis
Interior design: Kim Adis
Layout: Kim Adis
Photographer: Liam Goodman, except for p. 5
   and pp. 16-39 by Sloan Howard
Illustrators: Barbara Cottingham (p. 10 and p. 12),
   Phoebe Gaughan (p. 11 and p. 13), and Steven
   Fleck (pp. 222–225)

The following names/manufacturers appearing
in *Kenneth D. King's Smart Fitting Solutions* are
trademarks: Amazon.com®, FriXion®

Library of Congress Cataloging-in-Publication Data

Names: King, Kenneth D., author.
Title: Smart fitting solutions : foolproof techniques to
fit any figure /
   Kenneth D. King.
Description: Newtown, CT : Taunton Press, Inc.,
[2018] | Includes index.
Identifiers: LCCN 2017050115 | ISBN 9781631868566
Subjects: LCSH: Tailoring (Women's) | Women's
clothing.
Classification: LCC TT519.5 .K56 2018 | DDC 646.4-
-dc23
LC record available at https://lccn.loc.
gov/2017050115

Printed in the United States of America
10 9 8 7 6 5 4 3 2 1

DEDICATION

TO MY COLLEAGUE, editor, and dear friend, Judy Neukam. Without her vision and ability to translate that vision into reality, this book would not exist.

More than that, though, I dedicate this book to Judy's hard work during her years at *Threads* magazine, editing my articles and producing my videos. Judy has taken my fractured prose and crafted it into articles and videos that support my desire to convey information that is repeatable and reliable.

The sewing world has been blessed to have someone like Judy Neukam in our midst. Her tireless work has produced a considerable body of knowledge from a number of authors besides myself. We are all more knowledgeable about this craft, and richer, because of Judy. This author is deeply grateful to her!

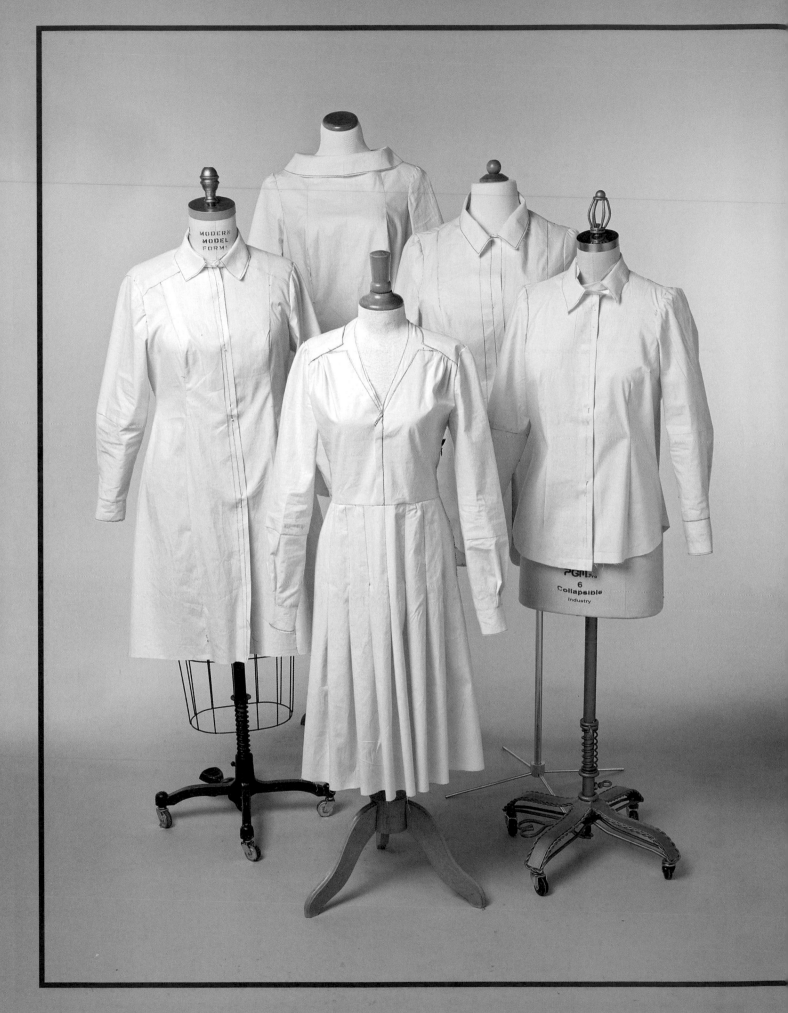

CONTENTS

INTRODUCTION

The mission of this book is to help the female sewist better understand the shape she has and the best way to fit it.

Clothes that fit don't have sags and pulls. Instead, the fabric falls smoothly away from the body with gentle form-fitting curves. The wrinkles in garments are like signposts alerting the presence of a fitting problem. Before you can make good use of all those fitting books in your library, you need to learn how to see what these wrinkles are telling you.

Tailors, designers, dressmakers, and seamstresses fit hundreds of people over a year. They are constantly moving the wrinkles in clothes into the seams to achieve a good fit. The experts have trained their eyes—and their hands, too—to know just where to take a section in or where to let it out to reach their goal.

This training involves assessing the body's traits, understanding the fitting options, and then showing the sewist how she can train her eye for what to look for when fitting a garment. Here, I explore the options,

interpret the signs, explain the causes, show where the problems exist on the pattern, and direct the reader to methods for making the alteration. I even suggest a few solutions for ready-to-wear garments.

Before you can establish a good fit in sewing, though, you need to understand where the fit goes wrong. I provide examples of ill-fitting garments and explain what they tell you about their fit. From there I explain my Smart Fitting method to make the necessary corrections for a greatly improved pattern that is comfortable and flattering.

PART I

UNDERSTANDING GOOD FIT

> "Garments send all types of signals to tell you the **fitting issue**, but you need to correctly **interpret** what you're seeing."

FITTING AND CONSTRUCTION ARE TWO DIFFERENT SKILL SETS. Unfortunately, the process of fitting typically ends an otherwise successful sewing experience because an understanding of a garment's fitting problems isn't clear. Often a bump, lump, or dent appears as a signal of ill fit, but the real cause of the problem is unknown. Many fitting experts tell you to follow the wrinkles because they point to the problem. But that's equally unclear, and my students repeatedly ask me, "How do you know what to look for?"

I've made a study of fitting throughout my career and have learned that seeing a garment and correctly reading the wrinkles, so to speak, happens by training the eye. Garments send all types of signals to tell you the fitting issue, but you need to correctly interpret what you're seeing. To that end, in this book, I will touch on several topics that will help you understand your own body and its shape, and I'll introduce some of the tools you can use to see and plan the basic form you're working with. Then I'll survey the various fitting methods. You may have fitting books in your library that use these methods. The information given here will improve the success of those books as your understanding of the issues improves. I will also explain in detail my Smart Fitting method, principles that rely on net loss, net gain, and no net change alterations.

From there, we will discuss making a muslin, or test garment—essential in working through fit issues. When you're armed with a muslin and background information about shape, the stage is set to demonstrate how to read a wrinkle and translate the information back to the paper pattern. Finally, you can follow the fitting issues of many different people and see how their garments have been sending them signals all along. It is my aim to give you the information and confidence to tackle any of your fitting solutions.

When the garment industry homogenized sizes to increase and simplify manufacturing productivity, the clear majority of the population forgot, over time, how to recognize real "fit" in the clothes we wear. These days, only custom-made clothes give you a custom fit. Even fashion is falling prey to compromising good fit and calling it style. We need to once again learn what a good fit means. As this book progresses, you will see for yourself what a difference a well-fitted garment makes in your overall appearance.

EASE

ALL GARMENTS INCLUDE WEARING EASE—the minimum amount of circumference (and sometimes length) added to a garment to enable the wearer to function comfortably. All garments have wearing ease built in; the standard wearing ease for ready-to-wear is 2 in. at the bust, 1 in. at the waist, and 2 in. at the hips.

Any wearing ease above this is what's called design ease, which contributes to a garment's overall silhouette. Commercial pattern companies have charts showing design ease amounts by name—fitted, semi-fitted, loose fitting, very loose fitting—and they make note of the ease name on the pattern envelope. Consider this ease amount when fitting a garment to appropriately duplicate the design's intention in your finished item of clothing.

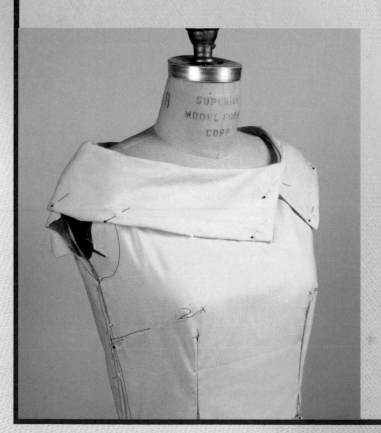

A test garment is the perfect place to audition the pattern's ease, fit, and style.

A big mistake people often make is overfitting. First, there must be enough wearing ease to allow for the movement of the body. Overfitting especially occurs in close-fitting garments. One needs to remember, however, that the person wearing the garment won't stand at attention while living in it, but will walk, sit, run for a bus, or reach for something high on a shelf.

This means the activities the wearer engages in are as important in the fitting process as his or her appearance while standing on the fitting block. This allowance for movement makes some compromises necessary in fitting. One example is the extra fabric across the back of an orchestra conductor's jacket. If there isn't enough room across the back, the wearer can't move his arms adequately. The judgment call sacrifices some appearance by adding room across the back with the extra fabric that it needs in the service of movement and comfort.

Day clothes generally need more wearing ease for the activities of life than do evening clothes. In evening clothes, the activity determines the wearing ease added. Generally, if one can sit, dine, and dance with a partner comfortably, then that's all the wearing ease needed. The rest is design ease.

A properly fitting garment hangs smoothly from the figure. Whether the garment has a close fit or a loose fit, it should hang with the lengthwise grainlines of the fabric perpendicular to the floor and the crosswise grainlines parallel to the floor.

Above all, the key word is *smooth*. A garment should hang smoothly from the figure, whatever the ease or fabric. The smoothness indicates good fit; the wrinkles point to the problems.

1

STUDY YOUR FIGURE

IT'S LIKELY THAT YOU DON'T SPEND MUCH TIME LOOKING at your unclothed body. Most of us get it covered as quickly as possible! However, we need to spare a few minutes every couple of years to make a study of how we're sizing up. All kinds of things change our shape—time, babies, weight, and exercise. These, plus lifestyle and occupation, can all change the way we stand, sit, and curve.

To help me teach you about fitting, six very brave women agreed to share their fitting experience. These ladies are part of the *Threads* magazine staff and understand the importance of evaluating the shape you're in as a prerequisite for a wonderful fit. First, you will learn how to abstract your figure and analyze it by comparing it to standard proportion guidelines. Information of this nature is the foundation of all fitting.

LEFT TO RIGHT: Sarah McFarland, Rosann Berry, Kenneth D. King, Carol J. Fresia, Jeannine Clegg, Norma Bucko, Evamarie Gomez-Bostic

EVALUATE YOUR FIGURE

THE BEST WAY TO EVALUATE YOUR FIGURE IS TO MAKE a *croquis*, the French word for "sketch." Croquis are commonly used in fashion design but also in garment sewing. These schematic figures are the basis of accurate garment drawings. A croquis abstracts your body and reduces the shape to the simplest line drawings so you can instantly see how the parts fit together.

To make the most accurate croquis, wear good underwear. If you're modest, you can wear a leotard. If you have long hair, tie it back so you can see your entire upper body. Place a chain around the base of your neck, and wear an elastic band around your waist and another at the fullest part around your hips.

Stand in front of a blank wall and have someone photograph you, capturing your body from head to toe, with the camera at your waist level. Be sure to get a front view, side view, and back view.

Once you have the photos, make your croquis by tracing your body outlines (one for each view) on tracing paper. Make sure you indicate the position of the neck chain, bust points, waist elastic, and hip elastic on the outlines. This tracing can then be photocopied larger or smaller and used to analyze your shape and different potential design lines on your figure.

THIS IS A CROQUIS. Photocopy a collection to use for drawing and experimenting with styles and to learn about your own proportions.

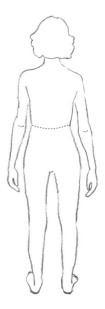

ANALYZE YOUR FIGURE

WITH YOUR CROQUIS IN HAND, it's time to study your figure. First, determine if there is asymmetry: Is one side of your body larger than another, or is a shoulder or hip higher or lower? This information is important for accurate fitting. There are other ways to analyze your figure. Although you can choose one method, using several provides more information.

VISUAL INSPECTION. Work with one croquis view at a time and begin to organize the information by drawing horizontal reference lines at the top of the head, the waistline, the end of the torso, and the base of the feet. Draw a second set of horizontal lines through the shoulder points and the base of the hips.

Draw a third set of lines roughly vertically, connecting the shoulder points with the hips. These lines show how the widths of the shoulders and hips relate. Use the lines to help determine whether you are balanced (hips and shoulders are the same width), have narrow shoulders (with wide hips), or have wide shoulders (with narrow hips).

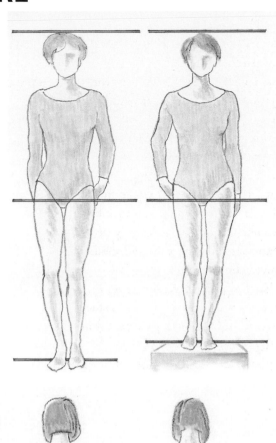

NOTICE HOW THE LINE DRAWS ATTENTION TO THE IMBALANCES? **These are shape differences that influence the fit you're able to achieve.**

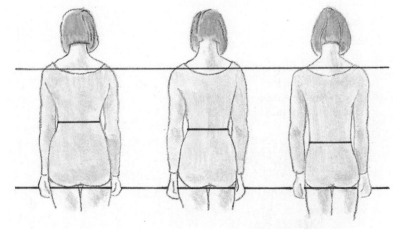

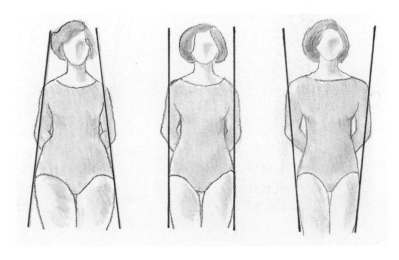

ANALYZE YOUR FIGURE

COMPARE TO "IDEAL" PROPORTIONS. Now you can use the information you've assembled to analyze your figure based on the "ideal" proportions of the human form. We are all part of the same species, and artists and scientists have determined that we all share approximately the same body proportions.

The height of the average person's head divides into the height of her entire body seven-and-a-half to eight times. Knowing this, in the "ideal" figure, the waist position is three times the head's height from the top of the head. That makes the distance from the waist to the floor four-and-a-half heads. Divide the head height by two, multiply that number by three, and the total yields the ideal shoulder and hip width (they should be equal).

Plotting these points on your croquis shows you where your figure varies from the "ideal" proportion and helps guide you to the styles that visually flatter your figure by creating the illusion of perfection. I will cover more strategies for compensating for this as we go along.

IDEAL PROPORTION
FOR ADULT FEMALE

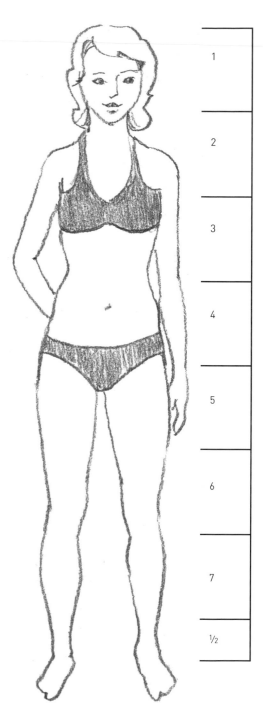

7½ heads high

1

2

3

4

5

6

7

½

Fashion Illustrations Are Misleading

In the world of fashion illustration, bodies are usually elongated to up to 10 heads. Highly successful models are often longer than normal naturally. Here's an example, using an illustration from a pattern envelope. I overlaid a normal croquis, and, using standard landmarks such as the waist, shoulders, arm length, and width, traced the elongated illustration adapting it to a standard body. Notice the difference? This could be part of the reason you aren't always pleased with your sewing results.

Use your croquis to sketch various styles and compare which ones work the best for your silhouette.

2

EVALUATE THE CLOTHES YOU WEAR

WHEN I WAS RESEARCHING INFORMATION FOR THIS book, I wanted to get an overview of the most common fitting problems to determine where to focus. I evaluated candid photos of lots of women and made an interesting discovery. Whether you know it or not, your clothes tell you when they don't fit and where they don't fit. The fit problem is everywhere.

Our models—Carol, Norma, Sarah, Rosann, Jeannine, and Evamarie—allowed us to photograph them in garments from their wardrobes. We found a bare wall, and over the course of a couple of weeks, we took phone photos of what each lady wore to work. Those are the photos shown in this chapter. You'll get the best results if a friend helps photograph your whole body and holds the camera at about waist level.

These ladies cover most of the general fit problems we see. They are short or tall, slim or plus-size, busty or not, and have different shaped derrières and curvy or straight figures. They also have a variety of asymmetries, with high or low shoulders, high or low hips, and curved spines. Most of the clothes you see are ready-to-wear (RTW), but some of them were sewn by the wearer.

As we took photos and started to develop a mass of examples, the photos began to reveal many aspects of the bodies we were studying. We discovered that after a selection of images for one person amassed, the clothes told similar stories about fit issues and body shape. And, surprisingly, it didn't take that many versions before you could tell which subtle details worked best to flatter the individual's figure.

Even though the images have been edited to very few, you will still see how each person seems to gravitate to a certain style. Some models wore knits primarily. Knits might be good for revealing your body, but they aren't so good at exposing fit issues because they stretch to conform to the body. Some of the ladies seemed to prefer wearing skirts; others pants. Even though our focus is on the bodice, we wanted to consider the whole body because of the importance of proportion. We could also tell by looking at the photos how willing the person was to maintain her wardrobe and invest time in making it look good. And I am still overwhelmed by what good sports these women are!

One thing is for sure—the body is not fickle. By the time you have finished reading this chapter, you will have a much better idea of the way your clothes send messages.

Mark the fit issues you think match yours. Later in the book, I'll fit these same women with muslins. You'll see their problems again and how they should be pinned in a fitting. Then, in subsequent chapters, you will learn how to alter the pattern to correct the fit problem. But for now, you'll have a chance to see how to recognize fit problems.

CAROL

CLASSIC BLAZER

FIT OBSERVATIONS

This jacket sends its message in very subtle ways, yet there is clear evidence that some fit problems exist. There are several examples of Carol wearing jackets, and they all point to the same problems but in slightly different ways.

Carol's body is asymmetrical with a high shoulder. Since the left shoulder is lower, the shoulder pad on that side could be built up so the shoulder line is level on both sides. This would eliminate the drag on the left side of the back as well, correcting two things with one alteration. If I were making this as a new garment, I'd make the hem level to the floor or have the hem slightly longer at center back. The sleeves look long; the back drags on the left side; the sleeves are too full above the elbow; and the whole jacket is slightly short in the back.

➤ To learn how to read and pin the shoulder wrinkle, see p. 76; adjust the pattern on p. 133.

➤ To learn how to pin an asymmetrical shoulder, see pp. 78, 83, and 141.

➤ To learn how to alter the sleeve length, see p. 82; adjust the pattern on pp. 131 and 135.

STYLE COMMENTS

Overall, the jacket is quite flattering. The sleeves turned back give it a casual look. The sleeve length could be a little shorter (by 2 in.), which would raise the eye above the fullest part of the hips, creating a more flattering line. In general, you should try to avoid having the sleeve hemline align with the jacket hemline. This can cause a strong horizontal line right at the hips, across the tummy, or at the waist—all areas that benefit from not having a horizontal line.

RTW ALTERATIONS

Because this jacket is slightly loose fitting, you could adjust the low shoulder with an extra shoulder pad. The sleeve can be narrowed in the seamline in the upper arm without getting into the armscye, and the jacket hem could be straightened up to the curved front opening.

BOXY LEATHER JACKET

FIT OBSERVATIONS

The strong vertical drag lines on the front indicate the jacket is too large through the bust area. The back has diagonal drag lines, and the sleeves are too full, but in different ways. The difference in the shoulders shows clearly in the back view. Notice the difference in the way each side fits. The short side looks sort of smashed, and the longer side looks folded. One calls for horizontal alterations, and the other calls for vertical alterations.

➤ To learn how to read and pin the bust wrinkle, see p. 79; adjust the pattern on pp. 132, 133, and 142.

➤ To learn how to pin a vertical alteration, see p. 80; adjust the pattern on p. 136.

STYLE COMMENTS

This is a severe style that needs a scarf at the neck or another soft, drapey feature to soften the look. Carol can get away with wearing it with a cowl or scarf because she has a long neck.

RTW ALTERATIONS

This jacket could be altered to be more flattering. However, it is leather, and the new seamlines will conceal the original seamlines if they fall in the seam allowances. First, the left shoulder needs to be built up, which will make the jacket hang square. I would try an extra shoulder pad. Reducing fabric across the bust through the princess seam will remove that fullness, and narrowing the sleeve, as well as pulling the jacket in at the side seam to create negative

space between the body and sleeve, will give a trimmer effect. You may prefer to take a leather garment to someone who specializes in leather alterations.

CAROL

PRINCESS-SEAM CROPPED JACKET

FIT OBSERVATIONS

Carol has the same problems on all her jackets—twisting in the back because of asymmetrical shoulders and possibly hips. Her shoulders are slightly rounded, and her chest is slightly concave. Her front may be a size smaller than her back. She has thin arms and a short waist.

➤ To learn how to recognize and pin a concave chest, see p. 78; adjust the pattern on pp. 141 and 144.

➤ To learn how to pin rounded shoulders, see p. 78; adjust the pattern on pp. 133, 138, and 147.

STYLE COMMENTS

The length of the jacket is good, as is the shape when viewed from the side. It's a fun style, and it would also look good with a full, sweeping circular skirt. The short length makes Carol's hips look trim.

RTW ALTERATIONS

Adding extra shoulder padding to the left side will make this jacket hang squarely. Also, some more shaping at the side as well as shortening the sleeve will make this jacket look smarter on her.

MAN'S SHIRT WITH YOKE

FIT OBSERVATIONS

I think Carol is standing naturally in these photos. She has a small top with a slight chest and square shoulders. Below the waist, she has an athletic backside and thighs with wider hips. Her shoulders and hips are uneven. On this blouse, it looks like the buttons were sewn on wrong; the shoulder slope is off, and that's causing the drag lines above the bust.

➤ To learn how to read and pin the shoulder slope, see p. 62; adjust the pattern on p. 63.

➤ To learn how to make a permanent shoulder template, see p. 62.

This is one of those garments that needs two different sides drafted, so the asymmetry of the shoulders can be accommodated. When the shoulders hang correctly, the rest of the blouse will settle in. Also, either a small side vent or shirttail will make the lower part of the garment hang better by accommodating the hips better.

STYLE COMMENTS

A white blouse is a basic wardrobe staple, and everyone should have several. But one caution: White shows fitting issues more intensely than other colors because the play of light accentuates them. The style is good for Carol and will work when she gets a blouse that fits properly.

RTW ALTERATIONS

If you sew for yourself, many of the alterations that make a blouse or shirt fit properly can be made through the yoke and never show. Because a shirt often doesn't have shoulder pads or lining, the wrinkles that signify poor fit show more. By changing the yoke, you can adjust the shoulder slope, blouse width, and arm circumference through the seam that joins the yoke to the blouse body while you have the shirt open.

CAROL

MANDARIN COLLAR

FIT OBSERVATIONS

This top works because it falls smoothly from the shoulders to below the waist. The high neck also succeeds on Carol's long neck. It looks like the darts were rotated to the hem in the design. This garment succeeds because it is cut wide enough through the hips and has no waist distinction; therefore, it falls straight from the shoulders, and the typical problems exit through the hem.

STYLE COMMENTS

This is an elegant solution for something easy to wear that flatters the figure. The color is restrained, and the drape of the fabric is very forgiving to any asymmetry of the shoulders.

RTW ALTERATIONS

Though the garment is a relaxed fit, I would shape the side seams to create negative space between the torso and the sleeve, giving the illusion of a shapely figure without being tight. Pulling in the front and back side seams by ⅜ in. at the waist and tapering to the underarm and hip will make a graceful, straight-appearing silhouette.

➤ **To learn how to add shape in the side seams, see p. 79.**

NORMA

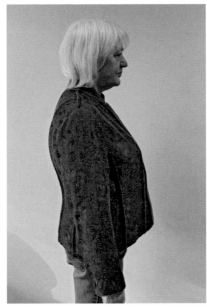
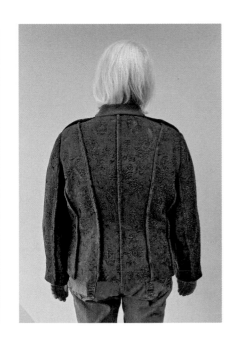

JACKET WITH VERTICAL SEAMS

FIT OBSERVATIONS

Norma has long, slim legs; narrow hips; a full, unsupported bust; and a wide, curved upper back. This jacket isn't sending bad fit messages. There are, however, some adjustments that could be made to make the garment more flattering without sacrificing its comfort. I would slenderize the back by changing the shape of the side princess seam to end in the armhole to help eliminate the full fabric under the arm. This jacket "wings out" at the lower edge of the front. If it were fitted so the front dropped straight down, it would be more flattering. Also, curving the side seam inward at the waist and then outward as it travels to the hips could create a better illusion on her figure.

➤ **To learn how to reshape the side seams, see pp. 79, 87, and 150.**

STYLE COMMENTS

This is a good line for Norma. It shows a hint of a waistline on the back and has slenderizing vertical lines.

RTW ALTERATIONS

The exposed seams on this jacket make it very easy to alter. You must be careful in removing the original stitching and cutting the excess seam allowance to keep everything looking original. This jacket can't be enlarged.

NORMA

ASYMMETRICAL ASIAN INFLUENCE

FIT OBSERVATIONS

Norma seems to have good mastery of fit for her body (she sews most of her clothes). I would fit out the lower ends of the front darts—the jacket "wings out" a little at the edge, just like the jacket in the previous photos. In construction, if you were to interline the entire jacket with a fine tailoring canvas, that would smooth things out nicely.

STYLE COMMENTS

This jacket is flattering. It appears that Norma looks better in a more structured garment. The color choice is also good with her hair.

RTW ALTERATIONS

A good deal of the success of this jacket lies in the fact that it was made for the wearer. It could, however, be fitted for someone else by making it smaller. That would be complicated but not impossible because of the multiple vertical seams.

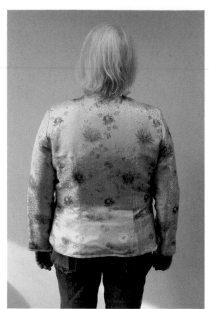

PIECED T-SHIRT TUNIC

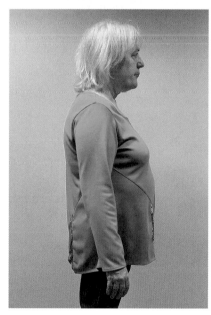

FIT OBSERVATIONS

We all have an occasional project that does not work, even for a professional seamstress. The fit on this top falls into a category where what you envisioned does not match the results. Several things went wrong in the design and construction. The tuck above the bust wants a dart. The bust should be lowered. Norma has narrow hips and long legs. This top camouflages her best figure elements. There are many drag lines on the back. Part of the problem is grain. She has drag lines under her arms, which could mean she needs to adjust the shoulder slope. The front hemline looks high.

➤ To learn how to relocate the bust apex and adjust the pattern, see p. 227.

STYLE COMMENTS

Here are some of the reasons this top doesn't work to Norma's advantage: The inset points aim outward to the sides right at the waist, which makes it look much larger. The diagonal inset in the front hem is inappropriately placed. The color overpowers her. Designs of this nature, while well intentioned, should be burned or banished. They don't look good on anyone, really. Shame on whomever drafted this!

RTW ALTERATIONS

This garment cannot be salvaged. There are no seam allowances, the grain isn't working properly, and the style is not flattering.

NORMA

TUCKED FRONT CAMP SHIRT

FIT OBSERVATIONS

Overall, this fit is good. However, the shirt is asking for more bust darts. You can see this in the folds on the side view. You could hide a vertical dart in front using one more tuck, and this would keep the front from tenting out off the bust. I think Norma sewed the side seams stick straight. Bringing them in by ⅜ in. at the waist, front, and back, and tapering to the underarm and hip will create the illusion of a straight silhouette that is more graceful. This is an old trick, one patternmakers used in flapper dresses of the late 1920s. Those dresses were supposed to "read" like a straight dress, but when this shaping was not done, they looked more like sacks than gowns.

➤ **To learn how to add fabric at the bust and adjust the pattern, see pp. 158 and 227.**

➤ **To learn how to taper the side seam through the hip and waist, see p. 87; adjust the pattern on p. 150.**

STYLE COMMENTS

The soft color is good for Norma's coloring. The vertical tucks down the front are flattering. The short sleeve length causes a line through Norma's bustline and across the widest part of her back.

RTW ALTERATIONS

A shirt this style could be altered through the yoke; the circumference of the sleeves could be narrowed, and the side seams could be reshaped if the result is to make it more graceful.

 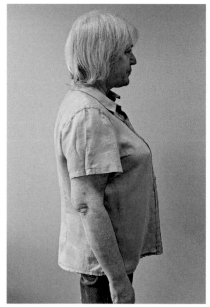 

***TIP* //** ALWAYS BE MINDFUL OF THE RELATIONSHIP BETWEEN THE LENGTH OF YOUR SLEEVE AND THE TERRAIN OF YOUR BODY. IT'S BEST NOT TO END A SLEEVE ON THE SAME LINE AS THE JACKET HEM. BE MINDFUL OF WHERE SHORT SLEEVES FALL IN RELATION TO YOUR BUSTLINE. IF THEY END AT THE BUST LEVEL, CREATING A STRONG HORIZONTAL LINE, YOU WILL WANT TO REEVALUATE THE SLEEVE LENGTH.

  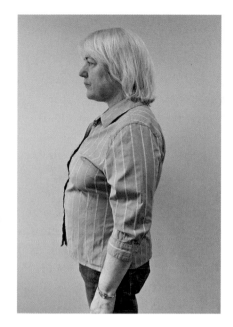

THREE-QUARTER-LENGTH-SLEEVE BLOUSE

FIT OBSERVATIONS

This shirt is signaling that it needs more circumference around the middle. The buttons are pulling over the bust, and the fabric across the back is causing drag lines. It looks too snug across the back, and there are drag lines coming from under the arms.

➤ **To learn how to add circumference across the abdomen, see p. 92; adjust the pattern on p. 150.**

➤ **To learn how to add back length and adjust the pattern, see pp. 153 and 156.**

STYLE COMMENTS

This is a much better sleeve length than the camp shirt because it falls between the bust and the hem. It also makes the arm look narrower. The back could look even slimmer by adding a yoke and a pleat in the lower section. For the least amount of alteration, wear the blouse open over a camisole, which will add all the needed extra circumference.

RTW ALTERATIONS

For this shirt, release the back vertical darts to give a little more room in the midriff.

SARAH

  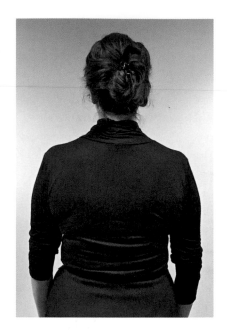

SEPARATES WITH TURTLENECK SWEATER

FIT OBSERVATIONS

It looks like Sarah is standing with her weight on one leg, but her left hip is high. The ripples around her midriff indicate the garment is too long for her body, so it bunches. Even though this is a separate sweater and skirt, the difference between Sarah's hip and waist circumference is slight, and the top rides up trying to satisfy a waist location. In a new garment, you would shorten the length in the midriff by at least 2 in. on the pattern.

➤ To learn how to pin a short waist, see pp. 54–55, and 99; adjust the pattern on pp. 162 and 163.

➤ To learn how to pin a high hip, see p. 100; mark for the pattern on p. 162.

STYLE COMMENTS

Sarah has a nice, full bust; a straight back; a short waist; and slim hips. She wears all her clothes well and does a good job of camouflaging her problem areas. She also has long, slim legs.

RTW ALTERATIONS

Sarah's left hip is high; this is easy to adjust in a skirt or pants with a waistband by opening the seam along the waistband and lifting the skirt into it. Trim the excess fabric so it will fit inside the waistband, and then sew the waistband back in place.

CUT-ON SLEEVE PULLOVER TOP

FIT OBSERVATIONS

This top sends many fit messages, but most of them are on the back. This is an area that frustrates many people learning to fit. The problem's symptom is not happening where the fit problem occurs. In this case, the problem is with the fit through the bust, and the garment is robbing fabric from the back to accommodate the front. This top needs a full bust adjustment and a side dart to make the front fall smoothly and eliminate the buckle at the waist in back. As it is, the front tents out, making Sarah appear thicker in the middle than she is. The design is intended to be shorter in front, but not that much.

➤ **To learn how to make a full bust adjustment, see pp. 97, 167, and 227.**

STYLE COMMENTS

When you see this top from the side, it looks like the front is full and the back is empty. It looks boxy from the front. Sometimes wide shoulders balance wide hips, but these actually accent the full bust.

The yoke is at the widest part of the back—I'd like to see the yoke continue to the front, and I'd narrow the shoulder somewhat. Alternatively, a boat neckline would be more flattering here than the oval; it would draw the eye up to Sarah's beautiful face.

RTW ALTERATIONS

This top can't be altered to fit Sarah without completely restyling it and possibly adding contrasting fabrics.

SARAH

JACKET WITH PLEATED PEPLUM INSERT

FIT OBSERVATIONS

The vertical lines above the bust are a common issue, and in this case, they are easily corrected. There's a princess line to the shoulder, so those wrinkles can be fitted out into that seam. If this occurs on a jacket that doesn't have the princess line, it can be fitted out into the armhole and the seam that joins to the side panel. The ripples under the arm in back are due to the garment's long waist length—there needs to be a little length taken from the jacket at the midriff. This will smooth out the ripples under the arm.

➤ To learn how to pin out the fit through the princess seam, see p. 99; adjust the pattern on pp. 161–162 and 167.

➤ To learn how to fit the midriff length, see p. 98; adjust the pattern on p. 168.

STYLE COMMENTS

The sleeves look like a perfect fit. Even the slightest pull at the bustline makes the jacket or top look too small. The pleats should be released on the back. Overall, this is a good line on Sarah. The front falls smoothly, and the length of the jacket looks good on her figure.

RTW ALTERATIONS

As described in the fit observations, the fullness over the bust can be adjusted through the seamline. The drag lines under the arms can be resolved through the back waistline. Again, these RTW changes are possible because the garment is being made smaller through these areas.

MAN'S SHIRT WITH YOKE

FIT OBSERVATIONS

There is a combination of issues here. The diagonal lines under the arms indicate shoulder slope problems. This is the first thing to correct. Then the garment body needs to be shorter—if you made a 2-in.-wide horizontal fold across the entire garment, those lines would disappear. There's enough circumference (the buttons don't pull or gap in front), so reducing the length of the bodice will make the fabric fall smoothly. The garment needs a side dart, as well as a shorter torso—not having them is what's creating the bunching at the waist in back.

➤ To learn how to pin out an incorrect shoulder slope, see p. 96; alter the pattern on p. 164.

STYLE COMMENTS

This is a classic white man's-style shirt. When it fits right, it looks spectacular. Once you have the fit corrected and a good working pattern, you can use it for any color.

RTW ALTERATIONS

Again, as with all shirts with a yoke (if they aren't too small), you can open the horizontal seam between the yoke and lower back and over the shoulder to change the fit, if needed. This involves sliding extra fabric into the yoke like a dart, then trimming the excess and closing the seam.

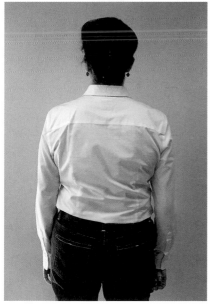

ROSANN

PULLOVER SWEATER

FIT OBSERVATIONS

A knit garment doesn't send you messages the same way one made from a woven fabric does. Instead, it exposes the shape of your body. In this case, Rosann appears to have rounded shoulders, a full back, a sway back, a well-shaped bust, a thick waist, and wide hips. You can see on the back view that the sweater bottom appears tighter than the top. The horizontal lines show the fabric trying to stretch around the body.

➤ To learn how to pin out for a sway back, see pp. 109 and 192.

➤ To learn how to pin a full abdomen, see p. 108; adjust the pattern on pp. 177 and 181.

STYLE COMMENTS

If this sweater were shorter, the illusion that Rosann's hips are wider than her shoulders would disappear. The length hits too low, which is not flattering to her shape. The sleeve length and width are good, as she has well-developed arms. Rosann brought several of these sweaters to be photographed, so they are clearly part of her personal style.

RTW ALTERATIONS

This sweater cannot be altered to fit Rosann. However, the sweater could be salvaged and refit following a current trend of cutting apart sweaters and collaging them back together in a piecework style, mixing in other colors, knits, and even lace or fur.

 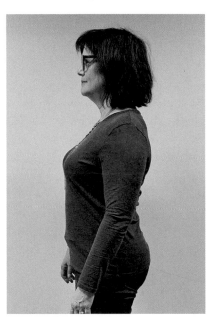 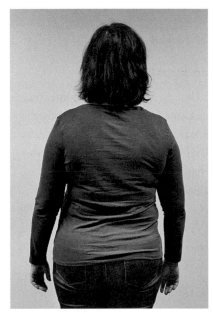

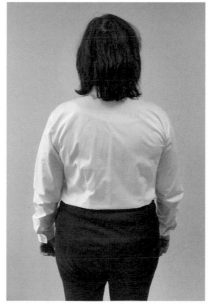

MAN'S SHIRT WITH BUTTONDOWN COLLAR

FIT OBSERVATIONS

There aren't as many drag lines on this shirt as we've seen with other models, but there are still problems. The signals point to the bust. The drag lines under Rosann's arms require shoulder slope changes. Adding a bust dart would also pull in the front at the stomach. You can see the shirt making its own dart fold in the side view photo.

➤ To learn how to pin this shoulder, see p. 106; adjust the pattern on p. 176.

➤ To learn how to alter for increasing bust fullness, see p. 176; adjust the pattern on p. 180.

STYLE COMMENTS

Rosann leads with her bust. Her blouse is asking for darts, which would eliminate the drag lines under her arms. Side darts, and even a narrow waist dart, would make this shirt flatter her figure better. Also, reducing the shoulder width so the seam sits at the top of her shoulder will make her appear to have better posture.

I would start over for Rosann with a yoked shirt, which would give shape to her broad back, narrow her shoulder width, and accommodate her sway back. There are back darts on this shirt, which work well for Rosann's shape. Another option is to have a princess line on the back below the yoke to better refine the shaping needed for her figure. On the front, a side dart as well as a narrow waist dart—or, alternatively, a princess line—will give the shaping she needs to accommodate her bust.

RTW ALTERATIONS

If the shirt isn't too small, these adjustments could be made if it had a yoke. It's much more difficult without a yoke because the yoke offers a horizontal seam across the back that makes the necessary alterations possible.

JEANNINE

MAN'S SHIRT WITH YOKE

FIT OBSERVATIONS

A woven shirt and contrasting skirt make a good choice for observing fit. Here, they tell us that Jeannine's right side looks longer than her left, and in some of the photos, she appears to be slanting. That is because Jeannine's right hip is higher and her right shoulder is lower. This shirt shows that the sleeves are too large for her arms. Jeannine has square shoulders and a slight chest. She has very good posture and a flat shoulder blade area.

➤ To learn how to pin a low shoulder, see p. 116.

➤ To learn how to pin out a long sleeve, see p. 118; adjust the pattern on pp. 194 and 201.

STYLE COMMENTS

This is a classic man's-style shirt that can be made to work for everyone.

RTW ALTERATIONS

For shirts like this, many fitting issues can be addressed in the yoke, as long as the fit problem requires making the garment smaller.

FITTED JACKET WITH PEPLUM BACK

FIT OBSERVATIONS

At first glance, this lovely jacket appears to fit, but notice the drag lines on the right side. Wrinkles under Jeannine's arms on the upper back and some sleeve drag indicate there's room for improvement. Look at how long these sleeves are compared to the hem on the jacket. Are her arms long, or is the jacket short?

Overall, this jacket isn't all that bad for the few problems it has. If I were making a new jacket, I would drop the waist by about 1 in., as it looks slightly high (generally the waist sits at elbow level). Then I would add at least 3 in. in length to the body to balance out the length of Jeannine's arms.

The excess across the back could be taken out of the side seam and back armhole. However, I caution against overfitting. This is a somewhat close-fitting jacket, so having some excess in that area of the back will give enough room for moving the arms forward. The sleeves look like they need to have the ease stitching adjusted to push the cap forward by about ¾ in.

➤ To learn how to pin long sleeves to shorten, see p. 118; adjust the pattern on pp. 194 and 201.

➤ To learn how to pin out a back that's too full, see p. 117.

STYLE COMMENTS

This is a very attractive jacket. The peplum back provides a curvaceous silhouette and, with the strong shoulder, enhances Jeannine's shape.

RTW ALTERATIONS

Due to Jeannine's lower right shoulder, adding a pad in that area inside the jacket will make it hang squarely. It would also smooth out the ripples under her right arm.

JEANNINE

CHECKED JACKET

FIT OBSERVATIONS

The strong vertical drag lines on the front indicate that Jeannine needs some more padding on the right shoulder to make the jacket hang squarely. Alternatively, a wider shoulder pad, such as a man's set-in tailored pad, would build the shoulder out across the front and back, filling in the droop that appears on the back between the sleeve and bodice. Also, some of that excess across the back could be fitted into the armhole and princess seams. Notice how all of Jeannine's garments are saying the same things.

➤ To learn how to pin-fit the side seam into the armhole, see p. 118; adjust the pattern on pp. 195 and 200.

STYLE COMMENTS

This is a jacket that serves as a good base for other elements in an ensemble: Pair with a pencil skirt and a white blouse with a high neckline and scarf or statement necklace.

RTW ALTERATIONS

The same padding methods would help a ready-to-wear jacket with these problems.

SOFT BLOUSE

FIT OBSERVATIONS
The cut and drape of the fabric make this blouse a success for Jeannine. The darts in back reduce fullness across the waist, adding to the elegant silhouette.

STYLE COMMENTS
This blouse is soft and fluid. Even though it is slightly large, it is feminine and looks nice. Slim people, like Jeannine, wear clothes well and can get away with incorrect fit easier than people with fuller bodies. This blouse works because it is soft and drapes over Jeannine's shape without causing wrinkles.

RTW ALTERATIONS
The yoke on this blouse offers many alteration possibilities because a yoke can be removed and the fabric taken in across the shoulders if needed. Be careful not to overfit a blouse like this, though.

 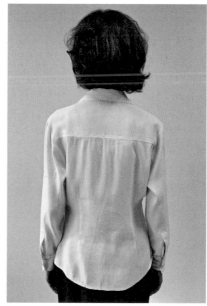

EVAMARIE

OPEN–BACK SOFT TOP

FIT OBSERVATIONS

Evamarie has a curvy figure with a full bust, narrow waist, and round hips and posterior. Most of her clothes look like they fit from the front, but the back side sends messages of problems. It looks like Evamarie is different sizes above and below her waist. She may even be different sizes front and back. The open back on this blouse doesn't look even because the back lifts to ride over her hips.

➤ **To learn how to pin a full hip adjustment, see p. 110; adjust the pattern on pp. 178 and 186.**

STYLE COMMENTS

The floral print combined with the floaty fabric helps keep Evamarie's proportions united on the front.

The twisted-drape detail at the back is fetching, and the peek-a-boo back could show a lovely camisole. The ease relaxes the fit, but the blouse needs more circumference below the waist to fit over the hips.

RTW ALTERATIONS

The ready-to-wear fix for this is to shorten the blouse at the front so it is roughly level with the drape in the back. Removing the fabric below the waist will keep the pulling to a minimum. The open back looks uneven because Evamarie's right shoulder is lower than the left. You can correct that by taking the binding off the neckline on the right side and lowering it enough to pull the fabric up, making the fit match the left side.

KNIT PULLOVER T-SHIRT

FIT OBSERVATIONS

Evamarie's hands are covering her widest figure element, so you can't see it from the front. She needs to fit tops so they are larger through the hips but stay slender at the waist. Knit fabric camouflages the fit (both good and bad).

➤ **To learn how to pin to shorten sleeves, see p. 126; adjust the pattern on pp. 204 and 214.**

STYLE COMMENTS

The black trim on this top is a good plan, but I would get rid of the black cuffs. Having the trim at the neckline directs the eye up where you want it to be. Remember that horizontal stripes give the illusion of width.

RTW ALTERATIONS

Sadly, there isn't a fix for this in ready-to-wear, as knits generally are constructed with no extra seam allowances. If you wanted to alter this, one strategy is to insert a vertical panel in the side seams of the bodice and sleeves. Using a dark color like black will do dual duty—it adds the circumference needed, and the dark panel visually reduces the apparent width, making Eva's figure "read" slimmer.

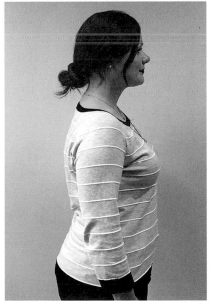

EVAMARIE

FITTED SHEATH WITH MID-LENGTH SLEEVE

FIT OBSERVATIONS

All of Evamarie's clothes look good from the front. You can see fabric buckling near the neckline in the side view. This is from an asymmetrical shoulder and improper shoulder slope. Her shoulders are probably more square than the dress. The horizontal drag lines across the waist are caused by her hips pushing the dress up to get more circumference. The bodice is longer than her body.

➤ **To learn how to pin shoulder slope issues, see pp. 62–63; adjust the pattern on pp. 204 and 206.**

➤ **To learn how to pin body length issues, see p. 123; adjust the pattern on p. 211.**

STYLE COMMENTS

Evamarie looks good in a one-piece dress. The color is good, and the zipper is flattering because it provides a strong vertical line.

RTW ALTERATIONS

This dress could be altered if it had a waistline seam. You could open the seam and slide the skirt up into it after removing some of the length on both waistline edges to shorten the waist and expand the hip. It would be more difficult to alter the shoulders.

 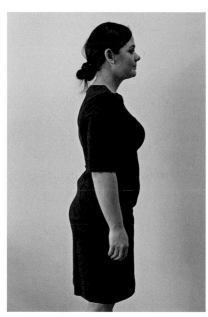 

MAN'S CHAMBRAY WORK SHIRT

FIT OBSERVATIONS

We aren't getting signals from the clothes because they are two pieces, which resolves the short waist problem. You could also have garments that are different sizes from each other. This could be the solution for Evamarie's fit problems. Separates are our friends!

STYLE COMMENTS

A straight skirt is one of the easiest garments to sew. Once you have a pattern that fits, you could make a dozen skirts for each season in no time and at minimal cost. And you can fine-tune the fit so there is plenty of space through the hips and to ensure the hemline is parallel to the floor. The blues in this casual top and slightly dressier skirt don't match, but the idea works.

RTW ALTERATIONS

This is a perfect reason to learn how to sew—you can buy separates in different sizes, but you can't buy a one-piece garment with different sizes above and below the waist and from the front to the back.

3

THE SMART FITTING ALTERATION METHOD

IF YOU HAVE CORRECTLY DIAGNOSED THE FITTING problem, the proper fitting technique will resolve the issue. There are different ways to get the results, but in my quest to find the Holy Grail of Fitting, I developed a process I call Smart Fitting, based on three basic principles involving fit-problem scenarios: An area is too large (which requires a net loss of fabric), an area is too small (necessitating a net gain of fabric), or an area isn't shaped right (leaving you with a no net change in fabric). In practice, the principle of no net change corrects for distortion after making a pattern alteration. These changes correct the pattern shape to reflect the figure underneath.

In this chapter, I'll walk you through the Smart Fitting principles of net loss, net gain, and no net change. The examples shown are in half scale to illustrate the different outcomes, but they aren't the only areas each of these methods alters. They can all be used in a variety of solutions. The changes are first pinned in the muslin test garment and then transferred to the paper pattern.

NET LOSS

A net loss shows up in the muslin as a wrinkle that is either vertical or horizontal. This wrinkle tells us that there's too much fabric perpendicular to the wrinkle—and it needs to be folded out to remove it. This is the basic principle. There are two different ways to remove too much fabric.

NET LOSS TAKEN AT A SEAM

The easiest way to take a net loss is at the seamline. You can take this net loss parallel to the seam, as outlined below.

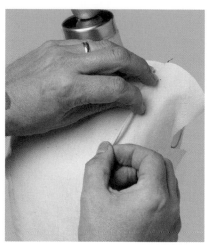

1. In a net loss, you remove fabric from an area of the muslin. This fabric can be removed from one pattern piece or from two adjoining ones. In this example, I am showing a net loss folded out equally along a seamline.

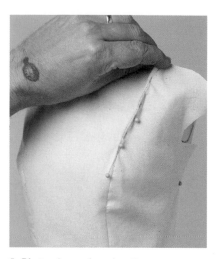

2. Pin to shape, forming the new seamline. Mark the pins.

3. Mark the new seam placement with a pencil or your preferred marker. Use a marker that doesn't disappear or rub off.

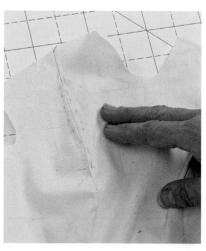

4. Unpin the muslin pieces to reveal the pinned alteration.

5. Open the seam. I'm using tiny embroidery scissors here to cut the thread and open the seam.

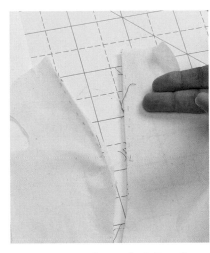

6. Here you see the marked alteration on the muslin, flat on the table.

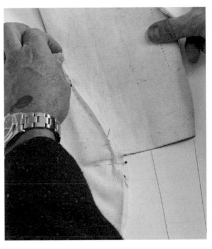

7. Align the original muslin stitching lines with their corresponding stitching lines on the pattern, and pin the muslin to the pattern. Slip a piece of tracing carbon under the muslin; then trace the marked correction onto the pattern.

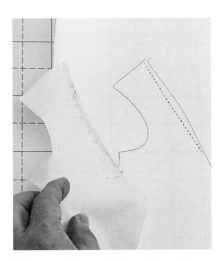

8. Remove the muslin from the pattern to reveal the marks.

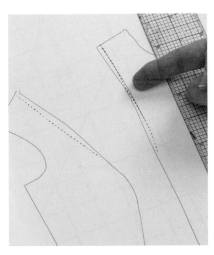

9. Repeat the process on the other garment section.

10. Go over the marking with pencil and ruler to make clear seamlines. This pattern is now ready to use and should fit the way you pinned the muslin.

NET LOSS

NET LOSS WITH A GRID

There are times when the net loss doesn't conveniently show up at a seam, but is stranded, like a desert island, in the middle of a garment section. I developed a method I call net loss with a grid to effectively make this alteration (and boy did I feel clever after I figured *this* one out!).

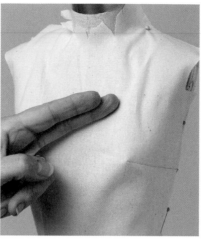

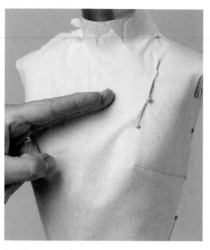

1. This muslin shows a vertical wrinkle between the chest and armhole, which tells us that there's too much fabric across that area.

2. Pin the wrinkle out, so the fabric is smooth.

3. Remove the muslin from the figure.

4. Make hash marks over the wrinkle with a pencil and remove the pins.

5. Here's the alteration shown in hash marks.

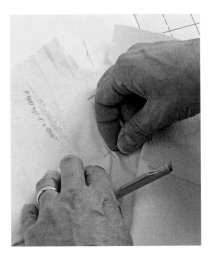
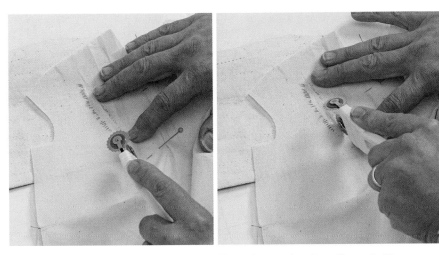

6. Pin the muslin onto the pattern, aligning the center and neck seamlines.

7. Place the tracing carbon under the muslin and trace the alteration onto the paper.

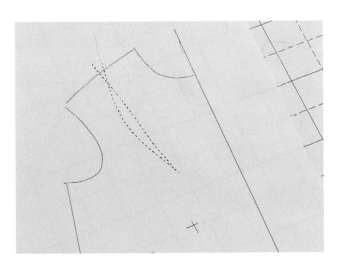

8. Here's the alteration. It looks like a double-ended dart.

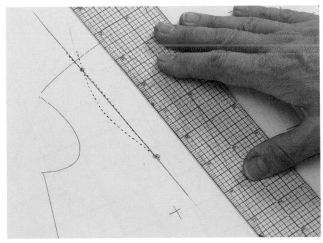

9. Mark the endpoints of the double-ended dart and draft a line through these points. I call this the axis. The dart shape is always an unknown until you've exposed it by marking and removing the pins. In this case, the axis falls on one of the dart legs, but sometimes it runs through the dart shape. Other times, the dart will be irregularly shaped. The purpose of the axis is not to mark the center of the dart but to provide a line from which other perpendicular lines can be drawn.

NET LOSS WITH A GRID (CONTINUED)

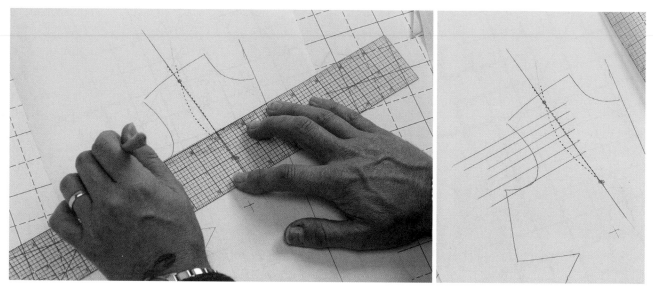

10. Draft lines perpendicular to the axis that pass through the dart and the nearest seam. The spacing between the lines isn't crucial, but ⅜-in. spacing is good.

11. Measure the dart width along each line and mark the same distance *in* from the nearest seamline that is not a centerline. You now have a series of points that indicate the shape of the new seamline.

NOTE: Since this is an armhole, I've intentionally drafted one line that hits the intersection of the armhole and side seam and one line that hits the lowest point of the armhole curve. This will be helpful later when drafting the new curve.

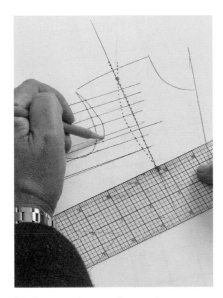

12. Connect these points to draw the new seamline.

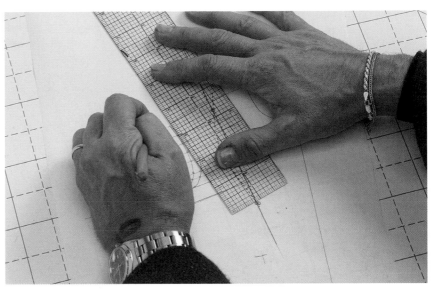

13. Now we need to correct for distortion. Since you don't want to change the original seam lengths, first measure the original seam length; then measure the new seamline. It will be longer.

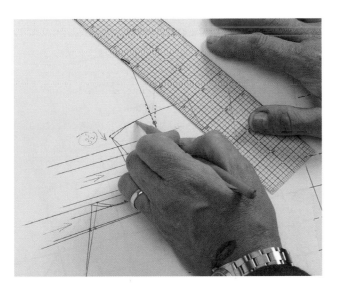

14. Since this alteration sits higher up toward the shoulder, remove the extra length from the shoulder end of the seam as shown.

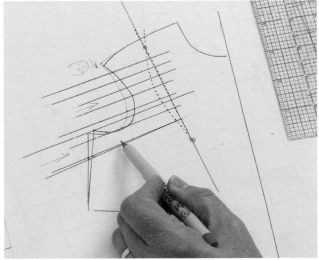

15. True up the seam and you're finished!

NOTE: If the dart sat down lower, you'd remove it from the underarm end of the seam.

NET GAIN

A net gain shows up in the muslin as a wrinkle, either horizontal or vertical, that tells us there is too little fabric parallel to the wrinkle. This most commonly appears either as a bind across the bicep or as a bind across the back. There are two ways to add to the pattern.

NET GAIN THROUGH SLASH AND SPREAD

There are times you need to add fabric to the pattern quickly, and the slash-and-spread method works well. This is the method I generally use when adding ease to the bicep of a sleeve.

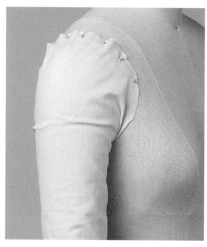

1. A horizontal wrinkle across the upper arm tells me there is too little length along that line, and a net gain on the bicep is in order.

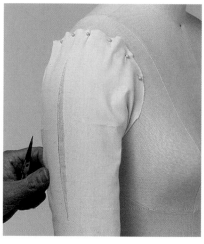

2. To determine the amount of fabric needed to correct the pattern, slash the muslin perpendicular to the wrinkle. The muslin will spread open the exact amount needed.

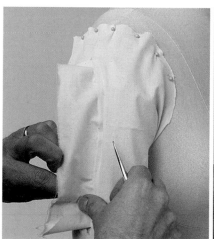

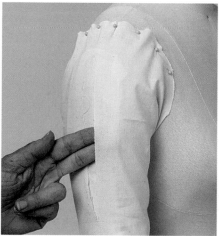

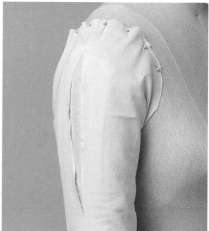

3. Slip a strip of scrap muslin under the slash.

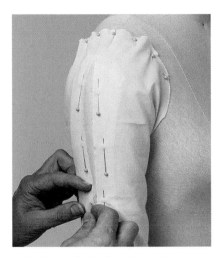

4. Pin the strip in place to set the alteration.

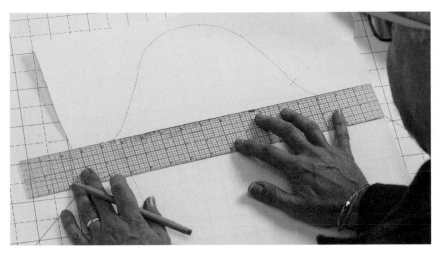

5. On the pattern, connect the two underarm points. This horizontal line represents the bicep line on the sleeve.

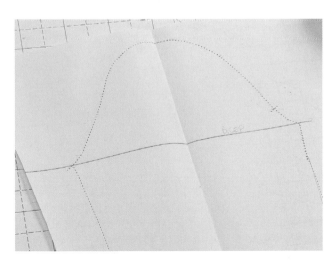

6. Fold the sleeve in half, matching these two points. This crease represents the sleeve grainline and its middle. Trace over this line in pencil.

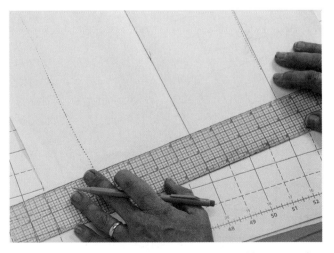

7. You can check to see if the sleeve is balanced by measuring the hem. The hem should be centered on the grainline. If not, move the two side seams until it is.

NOTE: If the hem isn't centered on the grainline, the sleeve will twist when sewn.

NET GAIN

NET GAIN THROUGH SLASH AND SPREAD (CONTINUED)

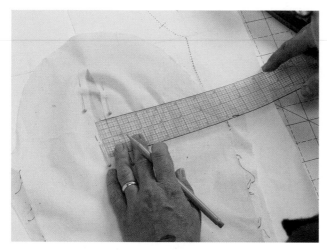

8. Measure the cut opening at the widest part to establish the amount of the alteration.

9. Mark four points on the stitching line: the top of the cap, each underarm intersection, and the intersection of the grainline and hem.

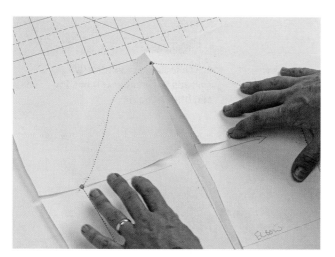

10. From the center of the pattern, cut to each one of these points. Cut to the points from the seam allowance as well, leaving a paper hinge to form pivots at the points.

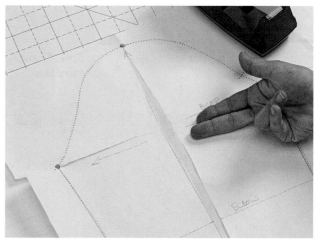

11. Lay the pattern on fresh paper. On the lower half of the pattern, spread the cut in the middle by the amount of increase you need to make to the bicep. Tape down the lower half to set the alteration. Allow the upper portion of the pattern to overlap the lower portion. Make sure the pattern lies smoothly with no wrinkles. Tape the pattern to the paper underneath to finish the alteration.

NOTE: You will notice that the cap drops. This is as it should be.

NET GAIN WITH A GRID

There are times when you need to add fabric to the middle of a pattern piece. The net gain with a grid method is effective.

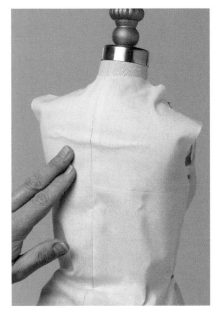

1. This is how the wrinkle looks across the back.

2. Cut the muslin perpendicular to the wrinkle.

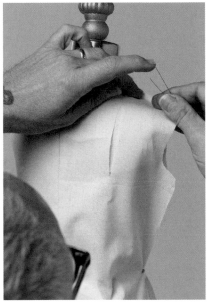

3. The muslin automatically spreads the amount you need to add (the net gain).

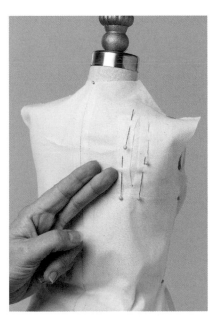

4. Place a scrap of muslin behind the cut opening, and pin in place to "set" the alteration.

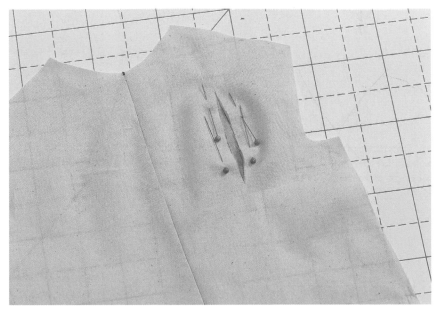

5. Remove the garment section from the muslin.

NET GAIN

NET GAIN WITH A GRID (CONTINUED)

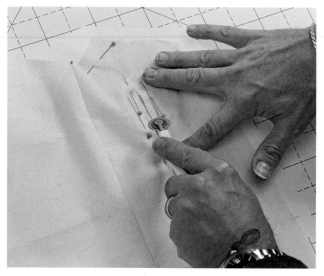

6. Lay the muslin on the pattern, aligning the center back and the neck. Pin in place. Then trace the cut edges of the opening onto the pattern.

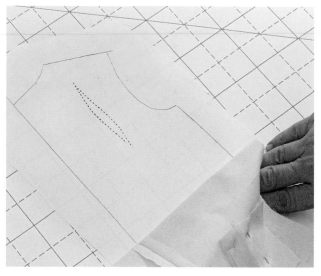

7. Remove the muslin to reveal the alteration. It will look like a double-ended dart.

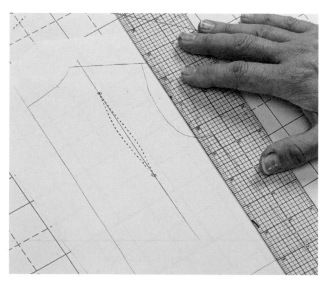

8. Find the end points of this dart and draft a straight line through them to form the axis.

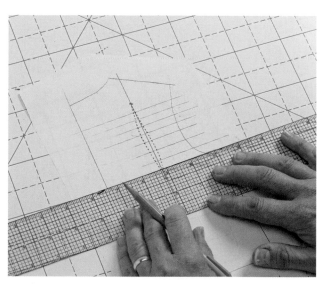

9. Draft the perpendicular lines through the axis, passing through the dart and to the nearest seam.

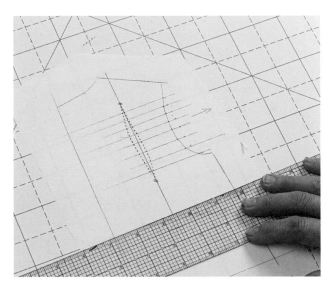

10. Measure the depth of the dart along each line and *extend* that line out from the seamline by the same amount. This is the same method used to subtract fabric for a net loss, but this time I have a net gain and am adding fabric. This is why the measurements are marked *outside* the original seamline.

11. A series of points shows the location of the new seam. Connect these points to reveal the new seamline.

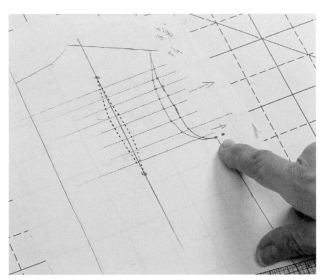

12. Now correct for distortion. Measure the original seam length. Then measure the new seam length. It will be shorter. Since you need extra width across the back, you'll add it at the underarm.

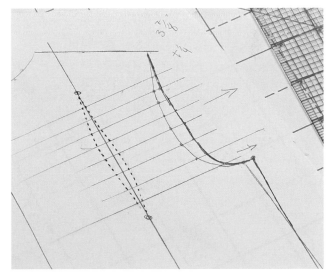

13. To finish the alteration, redraft the armhole to this point, as well as the side seam.

NO NET CHANGE

There are cases where there is too much fabric in one space of the muslin, but insufficient fabric in another space. In this case, simply move the fabric around, in a sense, making a no net change.

A no net change is the last of the outcomes in fitting, where we rearrange fabric within a pattern piece. This shows up as a wrinkle, usually horizontal. Generally, it is either at the small of the back on a bodice or directly under the seat in a trouser.

I'll use the small of the back as an example. The hang of the side seam determines if this problem is a net loss or a no net change. Pin out the waist excess into a wedge, tapering to nothing at the side seam. If the side seam stays perpendicular to the floor, it is a net loss. However, if the side seam angles to the back, a no net change is the remedy.

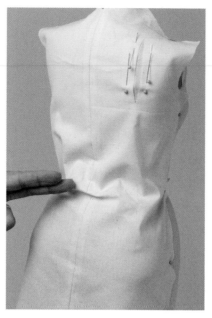

1. This is what the wrinkle looks like.

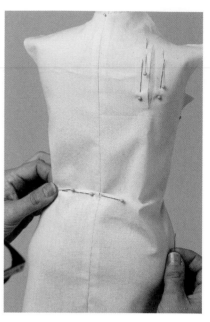

2. Pick up the wrinkle and pin it out. You don't necessarily need to pin all the way to the side seam; the amount of pick-up in the middle is most important.

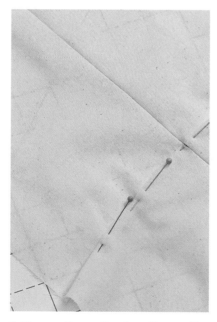

3. Remove the section from the muslin.

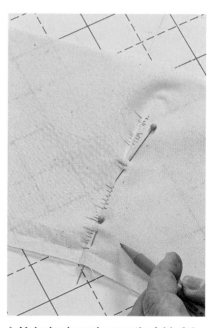

4. Make hash marks over the fold of the fabric to mark the alteration. Remove the pins.

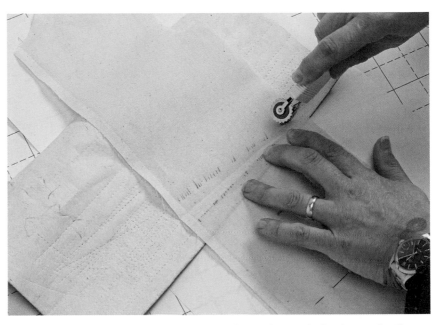

5. This is the amount needed to correct.

6. Pin the muslin to the pattern. With the tracing carbon and wheel, transfer the marks to the pattern.

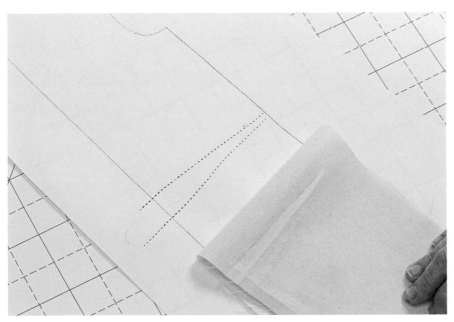

7. This is the alteration.

NO NET CHANGE

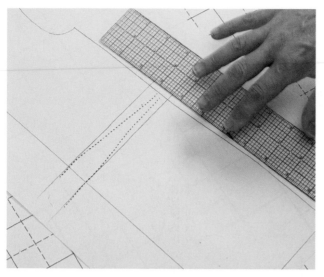

8. Mark two parallel lines from the widest points of the alterations, extending to the sides. Measure the depth of this alteration. You will need that measurement later.

9. Fold out the two parallel lines and tape them closed. This is only part of the alteration.

CORRECTING FOR DISTORTION

Once the changes are made to the pattern, you will need to correct for distortion, which represents a no net change of fabric.

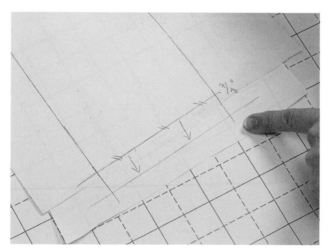

10. Add the amount you folded out at the waist to the length at the hem. This puts the side seam back to the original length, which you need to sew the back evenly to the front.

NOTE: What you remove at the waist you add to the hem for a no net change. You've rearranged the fabric instead of removing or adding.

4

MAKE A MUSLIN

IN THE PREVIOUS CHAPTERS, I HAVE SHARED WITH YOU the body shapes of our models, told you about my Smart Fitting principles, and expressed the thought that making a test garment (known as a muslin) is the best method to ensure proper fitting and pattern alteration. This chapter outlines how to make a muslin, including the tools and materials you'll use. Making a muslin is a fun and rewarding process, but best of all, it gives you a pattern that really fits your shape.

TOOLS AND MATERIALS

BEFORE YOU START YOUR MUSLIN, GATHER THE appropriate tools and materials. You will be cutting, tracing, marking, erasing, and marking and cutting some more, so get the best tools you can afford. Good-quality tools last.

Muslin fabric—Notice the *bolt* of muslin in the photo, not just a few yards. You will be using muslin like paper

TIP // TO MAKE SURE TRACING CARBON LASTS AS LONG AS POSSIBLE, COVER THE BACK SIDE WITH PACKING TAPE (CELLOPHANE BOX TAPE) TO PREVENT IT FROM SHREDDING.

towels, so buy a bolt. It's less expensive in the long run, so stock up when your supplier is having a sale.

Drafting triangle—Any kind will do, as long as it provides a true 90-degree angle. A triangle is helpful for squaring seamlines and for other drafting tasks.

Pins—I prefer the yellow ball-headed quilting pins for fitting. They are longer (which I find easier to hold) and inexpensive; the yellow head makes them easier to see against the muslin.

Drafting curve and gridded ruler—You don't have to get exactly these models, as other kinds work just as well. However, a see-through gridded ruler divided into 1/8-in. squares is essential for pattern work.

Tape measure—Measure the body before choosing the pattern size.

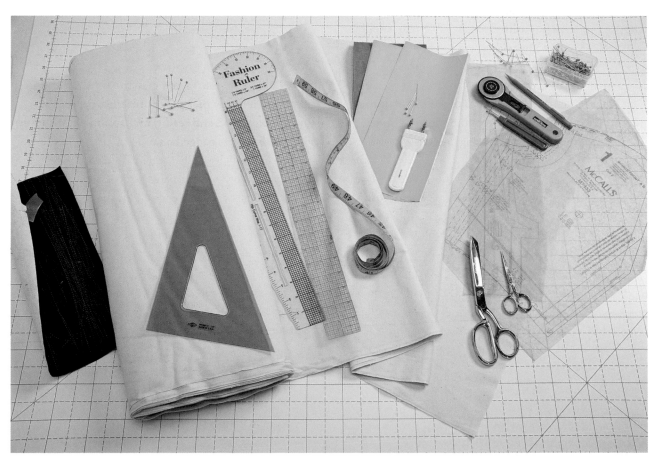

The tools shown will make the whole fitting process easier. From left to right: typing carbon paper (from an office-supply store), muslin, drafting triangle, drafting curve and gridded see-through ruler, measuring tape, dressmaker carbon paper, dual tracing wheel, shears and embroidery scissors, seam ripper, rotary cutter, pencil, ball-headed straight pins, and tissue pattern.

Dressmaker carbon paper—This is not the carbon paper you buy at an office-supply store. There are different types: chalk and wax based. Ideally, transfer marks made with chalk paper will brush off or wash out. Wax transfer marks are more permanent, but they are needed on fabrics with more texture, such as woolens. Warning: Always check the marks on fabric scraps if you want to remove them, and make marks inside the garment where they will not show. When making a muslin, don't worry about removing the marks.

Sheets of carbon come in different colors, are usually large, and can be purchased in college bookstores that have design schools. You can also find smaller sheets at fabric stores in assorted packages. Amazon.com® also has a good variety.

Dual tracing wheel—This tracing wheel is more than a novelty notion. It aids accurate sewing and is necessary to mark a muslin. There are two adjustable wheels on this tool. The width between them is variable. One wheel travels on the pattern stitching line, and the other wheel marks a cutting line. The distance between them determines the seam allowance width. I emphasize *stitching line* because I work from the stitching lines during this process, not the cutting lines.

Scissors and seam ripper—You will need two kinds of scissors: dressmaking shears for cutting muslin and short embroidery scissors for taking out seams in the fitting process. As always, get the best you can afford, keep them sharp, and you'll never go wrong. I like to keep a seam ripper handy, too.

Rotary cutter—This is handy for cutting fabric and paper. I keep two rotary cutters, one labeled "fabric" and one labeled "paper." Paper will dull the cutter's blade, so when I change my fabric cutter to a fresh blade, I transfer that blade to the paper handle and throw the paper blade away.

TIP // I WORK WITH SHEARS AS WELL AS A ROTARY CUTTER. DISTRIBUTING MY CUTTING BETWEEN THE TWO TOOLS MINIMIZES ANY CHANCE OF REPETITIVE STRESS INJURIES.

Pencils—Pencils are a personal preference. Some like a mechanical pencil, but my preference is a standard wooden no. 2 pencil. I have a heavy hand while drafting, and the lead in the mechanical pencil isn't strong enough. I break a lot of lead—and more ends up on the floor than on the paper!

Paper—Paper, like pencils, is a personal preference. There are different kinds, but my favorite is white kraft paper, also called project paper or banner paper. It is sturdy, inexpensive, and readily available in office-supply stores. It also takes rough handling and erases easily. It comes in 30-in.-wide rolls.

There are other kinds or paper, a favorite being rolls of medical examining-table paper. This is a thin paper somewhat like thin drafting parchment. Its advantage is in copying a pattern—it's translucent so the pattern is easily visible underneath. The disadvantage (to me) is its strength. It's too thin and tears easily.

A cutting mat—Although necessary for rotary cutting, a cutting mat (shown under the tools in the photo on the facing page) is also very handy for measuring, squaring, and establishing a true bias on fabrics. Cutting mats come in many sizes. I recommend the largest mat you can afford that fits your table.

PREPARE THE PATTERN

BEFORE YOU CAN MAKE A MUSLIN, you need to prepare the pattern for adjustments.

In the garment industry, there are three steps to patternmaking: the draft, where all the design manipulations are made before any seam allowances are added; the pattern, which has seam allowances, hem allowances, and any other information included so the garment can be made by the sample maker; and the muslin, which tests the pattern for any adjustments.

After you've decided on the size of the pattern you'll use, remove the main body pieces from the envelope, press the tissue, and separate connecting pieces from the tissue.

Before altering any pattern, I like to take the pattern back to the draft stage and add seamlines (most of today's patterns don't have seamlines printed on them, so you must find them). Measuring back from the cutting line by the width of the seam allowance is the easiest and most accurate way to achieve this. Mark the seamlines and hemlines. Marking the seamlines with the dual tracing wheel is not as accurate.

By going back to the draft stage, you eliminate confusion in the alteration process. You can see where the seams change and make sure that any distortion can be corrected easily.

TIP // THE ADVANTAGE OF MULTISIZE PATTERNS IS YOUR ABILITY TO CHOOSE DIFFERENT SIZES FOR DIFFERENT PARTS OF YOUR BODY, SUCH AS UPPER TORSO, MIDRIFF, AND HIPS. WHEN USING THE MULTIPLE SIZES, IT'S EASIER TO HIGHLIGHT THE CUTTING LINES OF THE DIFFERENT SIZES YOU'RE USING, REDUCING CONFUSION.

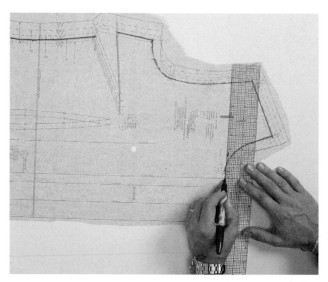

1. Measure back from the cutting lines by the seam allowance width (usually ⅝ in.), and draw the *stitching lines* onto all the main pieces of your pattern.

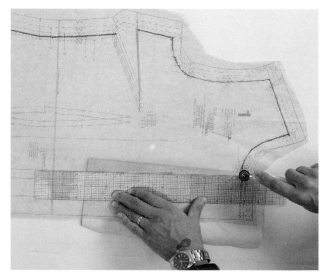

2. Pin the tissue pattern to a sheet of white paper. Two pins should do the trick; you don't have to withstand gale-force winds, just hold the paper in place. Slip your typing carbon paper, face down, under the tissue. With your single tracing wheel, mark all stitching lines.

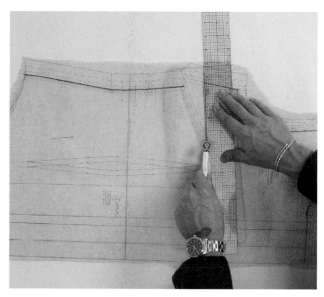

3. Mark sewing details such as the darts and the apex. Mark all matching notches by making crosswise marks over the seamlines. Mark the waist level and the line for altering body lengths. Be sure to transfer all markings, so the paper reflects any information you need to construct the garment. This converts the pattern back to a draft.

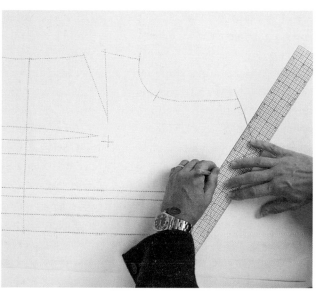

4. Remove the tissue pattern and put it away. Go over the carbon markings with pencil to make the information legible. With your drafting curve, smooth out all curves and use the ruler to draft straight lines. Accuracy counts at this stage!

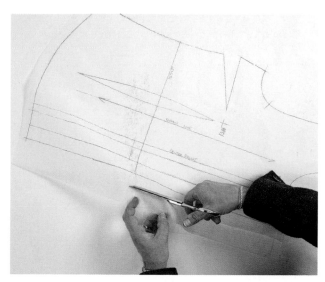

5. Roughly cut the excess paper away from around the draft, leaving at least 1½ in. around the perimeter to allow for easier alterations later. If you need to add at the edges, it's a simple matter of erasing a line and redrawing it. If you cut the pattern along the stitching lines, you'd have to tape on extra paper.

TIP // LEAVE THAT PAPER AROUND THE EDGES! YOU WILL USE CARBON PAPER AND A TRACING WHEEL TO TRANSFER THESE MARKS TO THE MUSLIN, AND TRACING A PENCIL LINE WITH A TRACING WHEEL IS FAR SUPERIOR TO FOLLOWING A CUT EDGE. THE CUT EDGE IS MORE PERISHABLE, AND YOU SACRIFICE ACCURACY WHEN THE TRACING WHEEL CHEWS UP THAT EDGE.

MAKE INITIAL PATTERN ALTERATIONS

BEFORE MAKING THE MUSLIN, you need to make several initial alterations to the pattern. These alterations are shoulder slope and body and sleeve lengths. Making these alterations before cutting and sewing the muslin can eliminate some fitting issues right away.

SHOULDER SLOPE

Since a garment hangs from the shoulders, look at the shoulder slope as if it is the foundation of a building; if the foundation sits correctly, the structure has a greater likelihood of being correct.

Therefore, you want to make a shoulder template. If corrections need to be made, they will be easier because the foundation is correct.

Make a tracing of the wearer's shoulder slope by taping a large piece of paper to a wall. Have the wearer back up to the wall with her weight evenly distributed on both feet and standing straight. Using a 90-degree triangle, hold one edge flat against the wall, and rest the other edge slightly on the shoulder. Make a slight pencil mark at the corner of the triangle on the paper. Move the triangle about 1/2 in.

at a time until you have a trail of marks that go from the end of the shoulder and up the neck on both sides of the body.

Remove the tracing from the wall and fold it in half, meeting the ends of the shoulders. Draw a line at the fold to represent the center line. Any adjustment to the pattern's shoulder slope, either up or down, will be determined from this template.

Mark in 1/2-in. intervals along the length of the shoulder and up the neck to create a tracing of the shoulder slope.

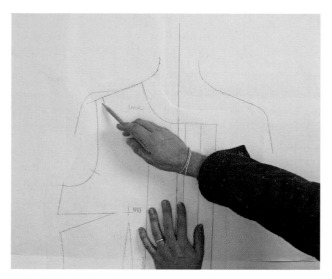

1. Begin by aligning the pattern center front over the template's center line (or parallel to the center line if the pattern is larger than the slope template). Slide the bodice front up or down until the high shoulder point rests on the shoulder tracing. You will see if the shoulder needs to be raised or lowered because the slanted lines won't match. I recommend adjusting the back pattern first.

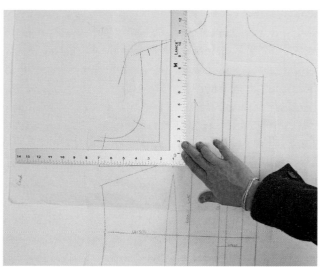

2. To adjust the shoulder slope, first draw an L-shaped line down from the shoulder line, turning toward the side seam under the armhole. Cut along the new lines to separate the armhole from the pattern.

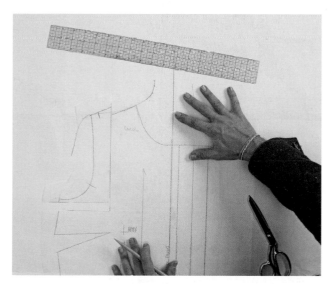

3. Slide the armhole section up or down along the vertical cut line until the shoulder end falls on the shoulder tracing. Tape into place.

4. To finish, draw a line connecting the neck shoulder point to the end shoulder point. Tape paper into the gap if necessary. True the side seam, blending the two parts together. Adjust the front pattern the same amount as the back.

MAKE INITIAL PATTERN ALTERATIONS

BODY AND SLEEVE LENGTHS

Correct the pattern's body and sleeve lengths to match the wearer's body. This puts the waist and hips in the proper position. When the waist, hips, and sleeve length are correct, you avoid other fitting issues.

The body length determines where the waist of the garment will fall in relation to the wearer. It is measured from the high shoulder point to the waist both in front and in back.

Make the same body length adjustment to the bodice back at the length line. After making this adjustment, check the back-body length measuring from the high shoulder point. Generally, the fit will be correct. If it is not, it is usually an indication that another shoulder alteration will be needed during the actual fitting. Repeat on the front.

After the shoulder slope and body lengths are corrected, check the sleeve length against the wearer's sleeve length. Lengthen or shorten at the length line, if needed. This will get you closer to the ultimate fit, but it can be fine-tuned during the fitting.

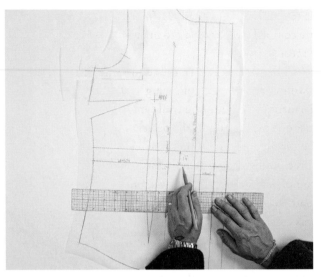

1. Measure the distance between the mark and the adjustment line, and draw a parallel line that distance from the adjustment line. This is the amount needed to shorten or lengthen the bodice.

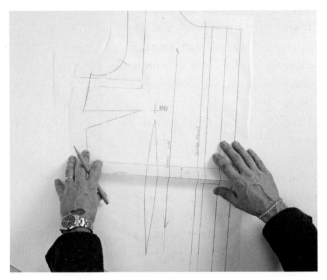

2. Adjust the body length at the adjustment line. To lengthen, cut along the adjustment line and spread the pattern by the necessary amount; add extra paper and tape it to the pattern. To shorten, fold out the pattern parallel to the adjustment line and tape the paper closed. On this pattern, I fold out.

BUILD A MUSLIN

AFTER INITIAL PATTERN ADJUSTMENTS are complete, you're ready to make a muslin.

As I mentioned earlier, the term *muslin* is another way of saying "test garment." Although you could make just one muslin to test the pattern, I typically make a minimum of three (and sometimes more for complex drafts), with each muslin made from the new pattern that was created from the previous muslin. Not only does this allow me to check measurements and refit as needed, but it also gives me an opportunity to make the second or third muslin from an inexpensive version of the fashion fabric that will be used for the final garment. This is an important step because different fabrics have a different drape, and some fabrics have more "give," which adds some wearing ease to the garment.

I understand sewists are anxious to get to the fashion fabric as quickly as possible. But think for a moment: If you've invested time and money into a garment that doesn't fit, will you wear it? I wouldn't. So take time to make the muslin, because a garment made from fashion fabric that doesn't fit ends up being awfully expensive muslin.

You don't have to make a perfect garment when making your muslin. You want to be accurate in marking and sewing, but you don't have to add too many details. Add the collar and cuff to see how the design looks. But leave off the facings, and don't sew the entire collar or cuff. You want to make enough of the garment in muslin to give an accurate read

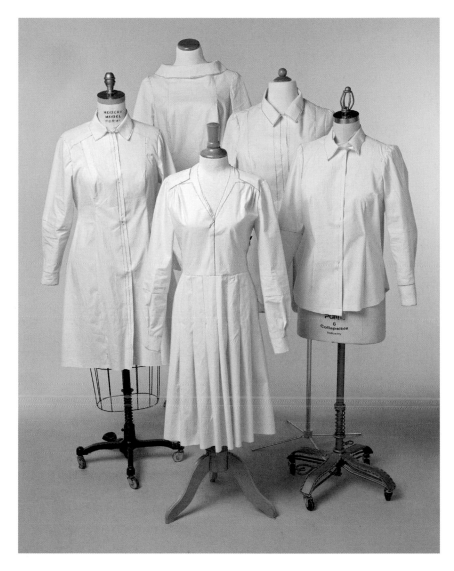

of the pattern for fit, but you can economize your construction time.

In the patternmaking program at the Fashion Institute of Technology in New York, I teach the fashion industry sequence of "draft, pattern, muslin." The draft is when students work out the design from the sloper (a basic pattern), with no seam allowances. The pattern is then created from the draft, with seam allowances, hem allowances, and any other markings added to get a finished pattern from which to make the sample garment.

I was taught by my couture patternmaking teacher to work in a different sequence: "draft, muslin, pattern." In short, work out all concerns—design and fitting—in the draft; then use the draft to make the muslin. When the muslin is completely correct and all changes are transferred to the draft, you can go ahead and make the pattern. This is the way I'll proceed here.

When I make a muslin, I mark stitching lines and cutting lines onto the muslin with a dual tracing wheel and carbon paper.

BUILD A MUSLIN

SQUARE THE MUSLIN FABRIC

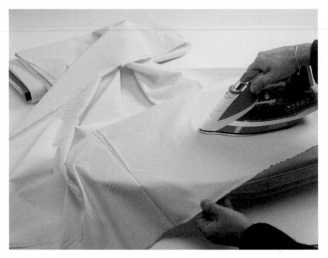

1. Always press your muslin before you begin. It's much easier to work with and will make squaring it easier to see.

2. To make sure the muslin itself is square on grain, work on a gridded cutting mat. Then find the crosswise grain of the fabric by "pulling a thread": Make a snip at the selvage, and pick up one of the crosswise threads from the fabric. Pull the thread gently, and it will begin to draw up the fabric. The goal is to draw the thread across the width of the fabric to the opposite selvage. This will be accomplished in stages.

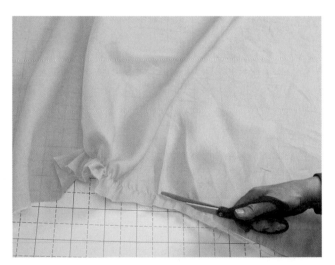

3. Smooth the fabric, sliding it along the drawn thread. You will see a line in the fabric. That is the crosswise grain. Cut along this line as far as you can, smoothing the fabric along the drawn thread as you cut. When you've run out of the drawn thread, pick up an adjacent thread and continue the process. Continue to the opposite selvage.

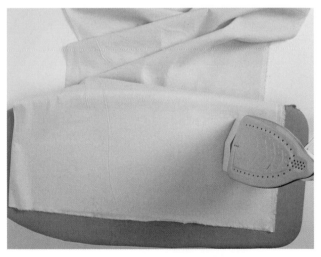

4. When you've reached the selvage, fold the fabric in half, matching selvages and the crosswise cut line you just created. If they don't match up, you must square the fabric. Stretch it diagonally to pull it back on grain. Pull the short corners and move along the long edges about halfway and check again. Eventually your fabric will be straight. Press.

LAY OUT THE PATTERN

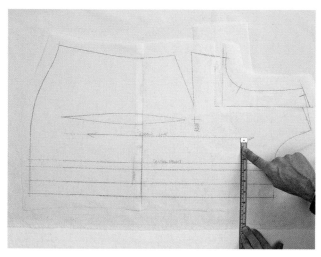

5. Lay the pattern on the pressed muslin. Measure from the selvage to the grainline at two different locations along the grainline to ensure the marked pattern grainline is parallel to the fabric's selvage.

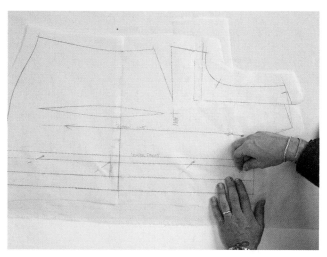

6. Pin the pattern to the muslin with a few pins. When pinning, pin well inside the stitching lines, at least 2 in. This enables you to get the tracing carbon under the pattern.

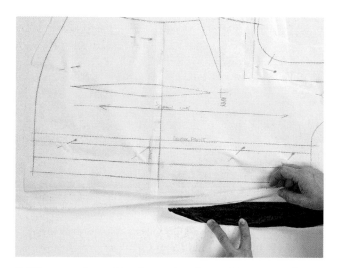

7. Place one piece of tracing carbon face up on your work-table under the muslin.

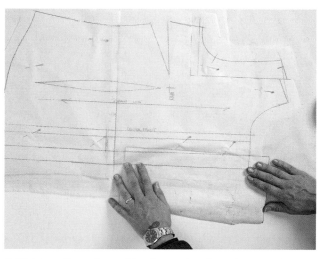

8. Place another piece of tracing carbon face down on the muslin under the pattern.

TIP // USE SHEETS OF CARBON THAT MEASURE ROUGHLY 12 IN. LONG BY 6 IN. WIDE. THE SIZE ALLOWS YOU TO SLIDE THEM AROUND AS YOU TRACE THE MARKINGS. THE LARGE SHEETS OF CARBON PAPER CAN MAKE A MESS ON THE MUSLIN AND ON YOU!

LAY OUT THE PATTERN (CONTINUED)

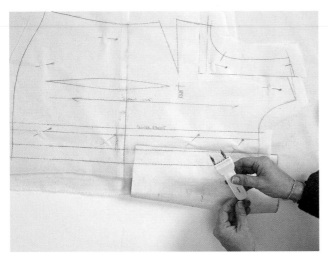

9. Set a dual tracing wheel so the wheels are the maximum distance apart. This makes the widest seam allowance, which you'll need to let out a seam during fitting.

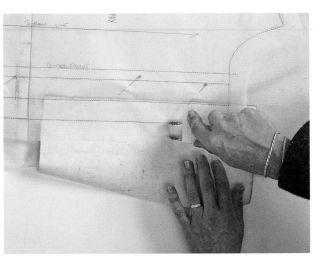

10. Run one wheel on the stitching line. The other wheel rolls outside the pattern and marks the cutting line. Keep even pressure on both wheels.

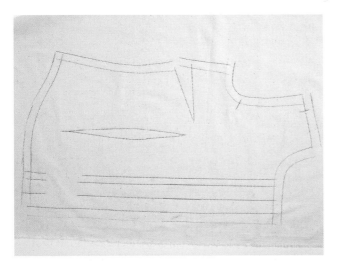

11. Work all around the pattern piece, marking stitching lines, cutting lines, notches, darts, and any other information on the muslin. Err on the side of marking too much information. Remove the pattern to reveal the marked muslin, ready for cutting. You can see here that both stitching lines and cutting lines are visible.

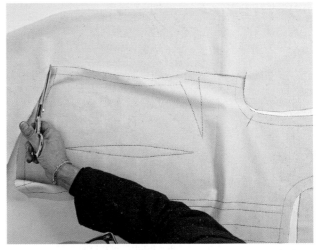

12. Cut out the muslin on the marked cutting lines. Repeat this process for all main pattern pieces. You're ready to sew your muslin.

A Word on Pinning

Debates rage about whether to pin perpendicular to or parallel to a seamline. Both camps insist their method is correct. However, as my patternmaking teacher explained, when you pin one seamline exactly on top of the other and then sew on the marked stitching line, you get a more accurate "read" of the pattern, not introducing any error through construction. Pinning perpendicular is not as accurate. Also, by pinning parallel to the stitching line, you can grab the head of the pin before it runs under the presser foot, pulling the fabric off the pin and preventing the machine needle from hitting the pin.

SEW THE MUSLIN

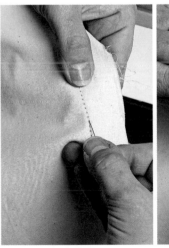

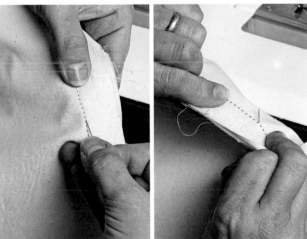

13. Once you have cut the muslin pieces, staystitch the finished seamlines of the neck edges, armholes (on sleeveless garments), and any other seams you want to reinforce, using a stitch length of 2.5 mm. Your muslin will also benefit from staystitching the center-front and center-back lines and, if you like, hemlines.

14. The next step is to sew darts or other details, but first you'll need to pin-baste them. This means pinning the stitching lines one on top of the other, with the pins directly on the stitching line. The pin effectively "bastes" the seamlines together.

15. Sew the garment together, using the longest machine stitch on your machine. This will make taking out a seam while fitting much easier. Check the guide sheet for the pattern if you need to know the sequence of construction.

BUILD A MUSLIN

SEW THE MUSLIN (CONTINUED)

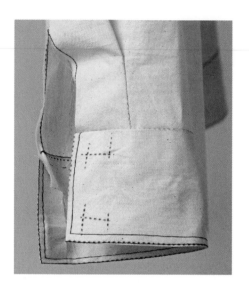

Collars This collar is cut in a single layer. You can see the tracing carbon marking the stitching line along the finished edge. Staystitching along the finished edge and then trimming the seam allowance close to the stitching is a sufficient way to prepare a collar or a cuff for the muslin.

A banded collar, like the one shown, is treated much the same way as a rolled collar. The flap and band are cut in a single layer, staystitched, and trimmed. Then the flap is sewn to the band and the seams pressed open and trimmed to ¼ in. before the collar is sewn to the bodice.

Cuffs A cuff is treated the same as a collar—single layer, staystitched along the finished edge, and trimmed closely.

If you'd rather not trim the finished edge, simply press the seam allowances back along the stitching line after staystitching. You'll have to topstitch them in place afterward, but some like this muslin finish for collars or cuffs.

Sleeves You can set the sleeve by machine or with hand basting. I find that hand basting the sleeve makes fitting a sleeve easier, because you can pull the stitches out more quickly when fitting. Since there is the possibility of needing to manipulate the ease stitching in a sleeve or remove the sleeves to get the bodice fitted properly, do consider hand basting. I think hand basting the sleeves is easier and faster, too. On the sample, you can see the stitch length I prefer, which is ¼ in.

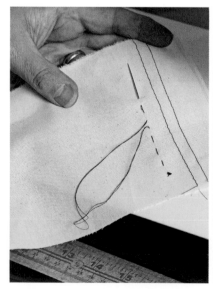

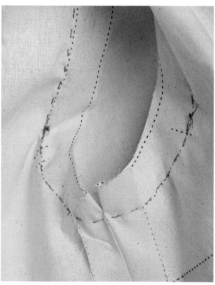

TIP // ONCE YOU'VE TRANSFERRED CORRECTIONS FROM THE MUSLIN TO THE PATTERN AND HAVE MADE THE ALTERATION ON THE PATTERN, TRANSFER THE ALTERATION *BACK* TO THE EXISTING MUSLIN PIECE. THIS SAVES TIME RECUTTING MULTIPLE MUSLINS!

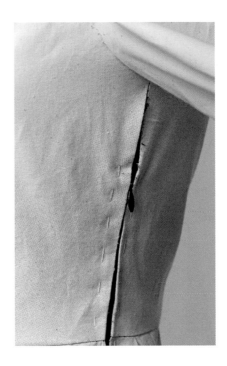

Zippers When installing zippers on a muslin, the goal is an accurate read of the pattern, not perfection. Hand basting with what I call "Frankenstein stitches" is fine. The installation of the zipper on the side seam of Jeannine's dress is adequate for a muslin.

Necklines This neckline detail on Jeannine's dress is another example of reducing construction time. It isn't perfectly sewn, but it's accurate enough for fitting. The neck edge of the band is staystitched and trimmed closely. The edge of the bodice and shoulder yoke that joins to the band is staystitched, and the seam allowances are folded over. The seam that joins the yoke to the bodice is sewn; then the entire piece is edgestitched to the band.

Other Details Any other details on the garment, like this cuff emerging from a center seam on the sleeve, can be treated in the most minimal way. You want the information to be visible, but the detail doesn't need to be accurately or completely constructed in a muslin.

Be sure to date your muslin and identify the pattern for future use. Most sewists like to change pencil colors every time they fit the muslin in future steps so they know which marks are the most current. In the end, you'll have a record of what alterations you made.

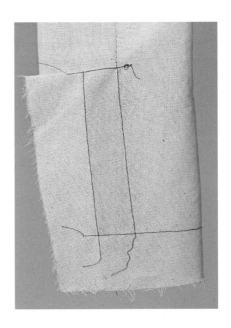

PART II

READ THE WRINKLES

AND

LEARN TO FIX THEM

AS I MENTIONED, I'VE BEEN STUDYING FITTING MY WHOLE career, and I've trained myself to know what a garment's wrinkles are saying. If you don't know how to read the wrinkles correctly, you won't know how to fix them. Our six models have selected different commercial patterns. I made muslins for them to show you where standard fit can go wrong.

Every time you make a bed, you get a fitting lesson. But fitting a sheet to a bed is easy because it involves shaping a flat fabric to an object. If you graduate to more difficult objects, such as covering a sofa with a drape of cloth, you discover it gets easier if you develop a method. Regardless of how easy or difficult the fitting is, the same steps need to be followed. In the sofa example, you first align the fabric's vertical center with the sofa's vertical center and smooth the fabric to the sides. Then you align the front edge with the floor and smooth the fabric up, across the seat, over the back, and down. Tuck everything into the cracks, and what was a flat fabric is now a slipcover.

Fitting a slipcover is so much like fitting a garment that I wonder why it is such a stumbling block for many sewists. I know you frustrated fitters well; you have many fitting books, but you're still not satisfied with the results you get when fitting. You might even give up garment making and take up quilting.

Wait a minute! It's possible you're fitting in the wrong places. You'll never get the results you want until you learn how to read a wrinkle.

Clothes that fit don't have sags and pulls, and the wrinkles are like signposts alerting you to the presence of a fitting problem. Before you can make good use of all those fitting books, you need to first learn what these wrinkles are telling you.

Most of the time, people are troubled by the same fit problems from garment to garment. In the following chapters, one model at a time, you will see how the fit starts coming together when the wrinkles are pinned out. Compare the issues with the fit problems you saw on the same models in their candid photographs in Part I.

CAROL

Carol chose a classic shirt pattern without a yoke. When I created the muslin, I made preliminary alterations for Carol's high right shoulder and short torso, as was recommended in Part I, chapter 2. Now we are going to read the muslin and learn what it is telling us.

FIRST FITTING: IDENTIFY THE WRINKLES

Start at the garment top and work down the body. On the front, notice how the collar sits away from Carol's neck, which isn't quite what this style calls for. Also, there are different drag lines from the collar to the lower armscye. And her low left shoulder creates a diagonal drag.

FRONT There's a fullness in the fabric across the bust, which shows up in the position of the armhole. The armhole sits too far away from center, not as close as it should be for her figure.

LEFT SIDE You can clearly see the issues affecting the fit from the left side. The shoulder is too low on the arm. The vertical ripples that show on either side of the sleeve indicate excess fabric across both the front and back. The horizontal ripple, or drag line under the arm, is the result of a low shoulder. And the slanting ripple traveling diagonally from the apex down toward the side seam indicates improper apex placement. The darts on the shirt are positioned too low for Carol's bust placement.

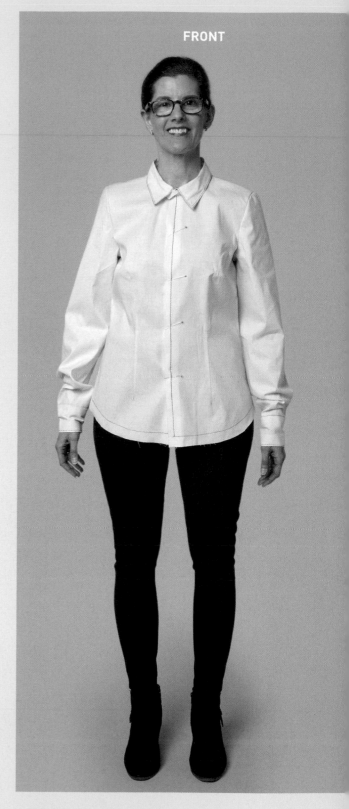

FRONT

BACK From the back, you can see the diagonal drag line rising from Carol's hip to her right shoulder. With this information, the garment says to adjust the left shoulder to make the shirt hang squarely.

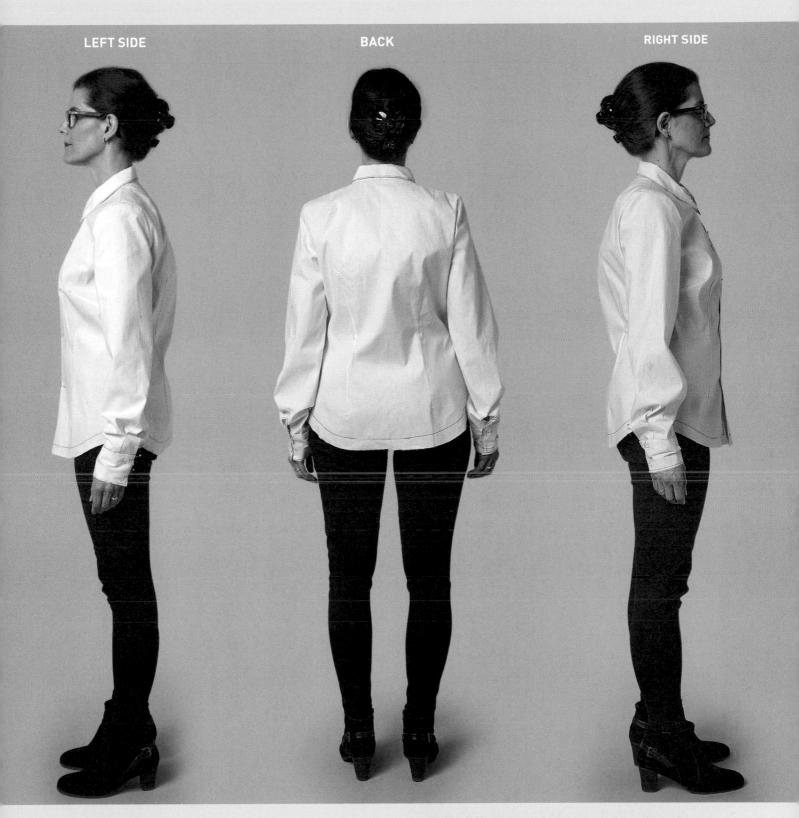

UPPER BACK You can also see that the shirt is too wide across the upper back, causing the shoulder to end too low down on the arm—especially on the left side. You can see a vertical ripple on the back that is parallel with the armhole.

RIGHT SIDE On the right side, you can see the excess fabric across the bust and upper chest area, which appears as a ripple on Carol's right side. The armhole sits too far from the neck, not at the top of the shoulder, where it should be.

PIN OUT THE WRINKLES

LOW SHOULDER

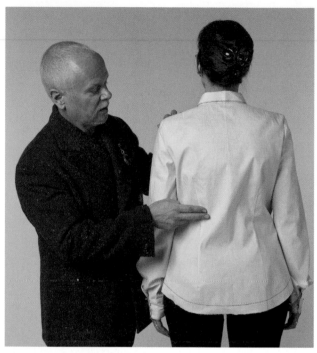

1. Before any other alterations can continue, the garment needs to be hanging squarely from the shoulders to remove the diagonal drag line.

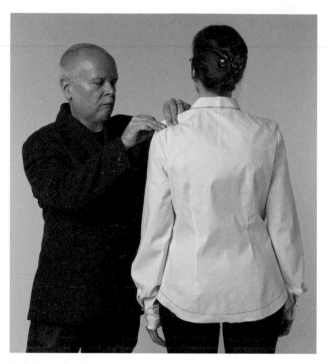

2. Pull up the fabric until the diagonal drag line on the back disappears. Pin out the excess equally, front and back, at the shoulder seam. This is a net loss of fabric on the left side only.

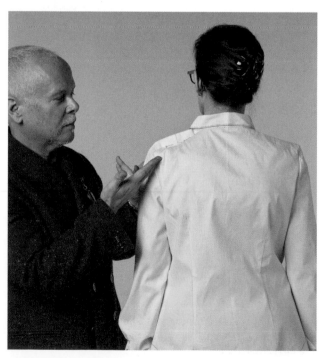

3. This net loss will extend up into the collar, reducing the circumference on the left side.

TIP // THE DRAG LINE POINTS TO THE *HIGHER* SHOULDER—IN THIS CASE, CAROL'S RIGHT SHOULDER. THEREFORE, THE LEFT SHOULDER IS LOWER.

A Low Shoulder in a Tailored Garment

In non-tailored garments, I fit to the higher shoulder slope to eliminate the drag lines, achieve proper fit, and make the garment hang smoothly. Then I adjust the lower shoulder.

When fitting a tailored jacket with padded shoulders, I fit to the higher shoulder slope and the lower underarm. I add more padding to the lower shoulder to make both sides level, then fit the muslin. Fitting to the lower underarm for both sides eliminates the diagonal drag lines under the arm on the lower side.

WIDE BACK AND NECKLINE

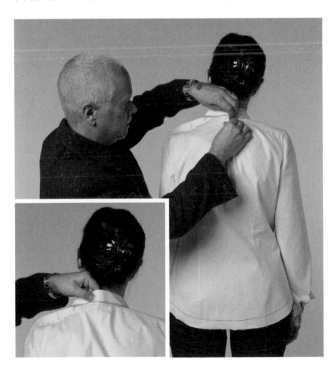

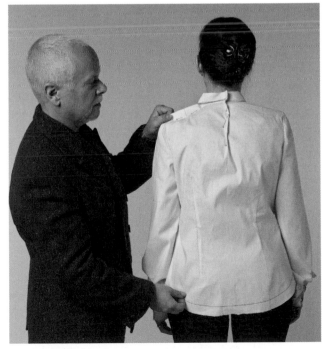

1. There is too much width at the center back, which causes the collar to gap away from Carol's neck and the shoulder end to be too far away from the center. To correct the shoulders, adjust the neck first to pull the shoulder seam up into the proper position. This alteration is a net loss, reducing the back width from the neck down to the hem.

2. My solution was to pin at the center back, reducing the width at the neck, and across the upper shoulder area. This is a net loss, as I will remove fabric from the pattern. This alteration tapers to zero at the hem of the shirt, but it is pinned at the upper body to anchor the shoulders for the next alteration.

PIN OUT THE WRINKLES

SHOULDERS ROTATE FORWARD

1. Carol's shoulders rotate forward, which causes a concave chest and a ripple between her shoulder joint and rib cage. Another indicator of this is when the armhole seam travels away from the bodice and onto the arm. I will correct this with a net loss of fabric in this area.

2. I pinned out the excess in a double-ended dart shape on the right side, which pulls the armhole seam into the proper position. The fabric now lies smoothly across this area.

ASYMMETRICAL SHOULDERS

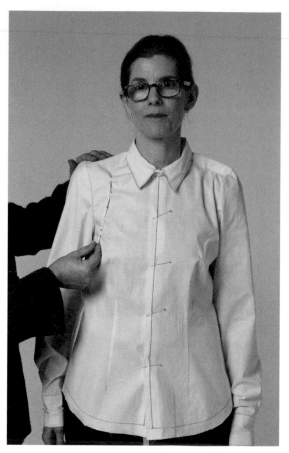

1. Carol's left side has more vertical ripples than the right, which means two separate alterations will be needed. The right side is easier to correct in the initial muslin, but I'll need to make refinements to the left side in the next muslin for the asymmetrical shoulders.

SLIGHT BUST

1. Check the bust area. The first thing I noticed is that the apex and dart ends are too low for Carol's bust. You can see this by the ripple I'm pointing out. Correcting this issue will be a no net change in the pattern. Carol has the right amount of ease across the bust.

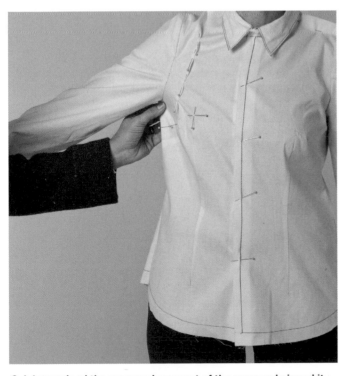

2. I determined the proper placement of the apex and pinned it with intersecting pins. Also, I pinned a line to show where the dart placement needs to be. Pinching out under the arm, I see that Carol has enough circumference in the bust.

WAISTLINE

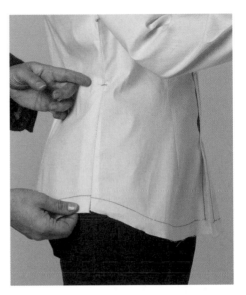

1. The mark at the waist shows me that the pattern length matches Carol's waist length. As mentioned previously, I made a preliminary alteration to the pattern to accommodate Carol's short waist before I made the muslin.

TIP // IN LOOSE-FITTING RTW GARMENTS SUCH AS THIS SHIRT, ONE SEES A STRAIGHT SIDE SEAM. TO CREATE A GRACEFUL GARMENT THAT STILL "READS" LIKE A STRAIGHT SILHOUETTE, DRAFT A STRAIGHT LINE (FRONT AND BACK) FROM THE UNDERARM TO THE HEM. AT THE WAIST: MEASURE IN 3/8 IN. AND DRAFT A SMOOTH CURVE FROM UNDERARM TO WAIST TO HEM. THIS GIVES YOU A GARMENT THAT LOOKS LIKE A GARMENT, NOT A BURLAP BAG.

PIN OUT THE WRINKLES

VERTICAL SEAMS

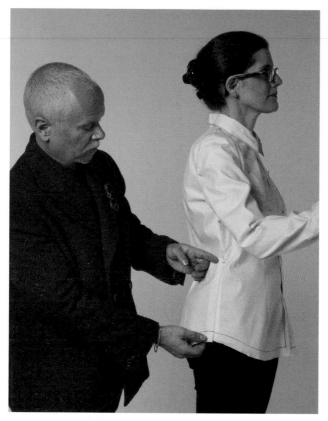

1. The side seam angles toward the back, caused by insufficient circumference across the hip. Correcting the issue is a net gain of fabric.

2. To adjust the circumference, I took out the stitching on the seam up to the waist. Then I let out the back seam, tapering to nothing at the waist, and overlapped it onto the front, which I took in slightly. Now the seam sits square to the floor.

Warning when Pinning Out Circumferences

Garments need to move in the real world, and you need some wearing ease to accommodate that. There is such a thing as overfitting. Whenever you have a net loss and need to remove fabric, particularly when pinning out a circumference, don't be too aggressive.

The actress Mae West had two costumes for her film scenes. There was the costume for the long shot, which had absolutely no wearing ease. She couldn't bend at the waist or move around much, but she looked *fabulous*. She would change her costume into a version with the proper wearing ease when she needed to move around.

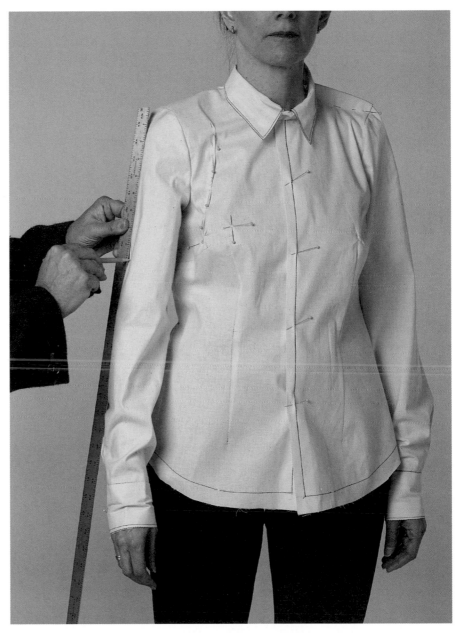

SLEEVE GRAINLINES

1. Checking the grainline on a sleeve isn't as crucial for a shirt as it is for a tailored jacket, but it should be checked, especially if you have changed the sleeve position.

2. After fitting the sleeve to the proper pitch, establish a new grainline by hanging a ruler plumb to the floor, then drawing a grainline on the sleeve. Change the grainline on the pattern before cutting the fashion fabric. This is a no net change.

PIN OUT THE WRINKLES

SLEEVE LENGTH

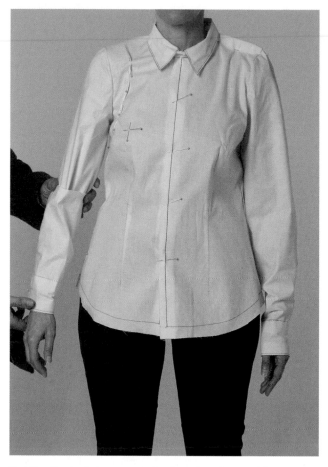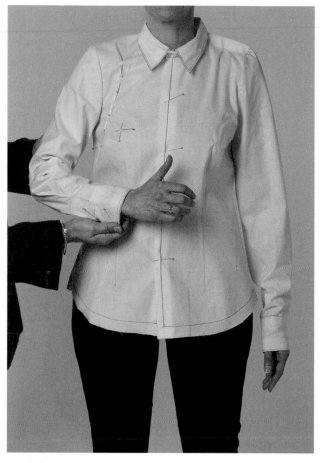

1. After the body is corrected, adjust the sleeves. The sleeve on this pattern is too long for Carol, so shortening it will be a net loss.

There are two ways to adjust length on a sleeve. The first way is to simply fold the cuff back to determine how much to alter. If the sleeve is cut straight, this won't affect the diameter of the cuff. However, if you wish to retain the diameter of the cuff, remove the excess length by folding it out in the sleeve body. For either way, be sure to account for the depth of the cuff when adjusting the sleeve length.

Although sleeve length is a personal preference, the convention is that when the arm is bent at a 90-degree angle, the edge of the cuff should sit at the base of the wrist joint, covering the prominent bone.

2. Finally, check the sleeve for range of motion. Since this is a tailored man's shirt, it needs more range of motion than a dressy blouse does.

TIP // IN THE CASE OF TAILORED GARMENTS THAT HAVE A SLEEVE WITH AN ELBOW DART, OR A TWO-PART TAILORED SLEEVE, YOU ALTER THE SLEEVE BOTH ABOVE THE ELBOW AND BELOW. OTHERWISE, THE BEND OF THE SLEEVE WON'T REFLECT THE WEARER'S ELBOW.

THE PINNED-OUT MUSLIN

Take a look at the muslin now that it has been pinned. From here, the corrections will be marked on the muslin, the paper pattern will be adjusted, and then either a second muslin or an edited first muslin will be fitted again, which you will see in Part III.

NORMA

Norma's pattern is a long-sleeved button-front tunic with vertical seams and a collar. When preparing Norma's pattern, I made a full bust adjustment to the pattern to accommodate her full bust. For more on this, see p. 227. The need to do this showed up when I was checking the front and back lengths—the front was shorter than Norma's measurement. When alteration needs are obvious, making them before creating a muslin will provide a better starting place, bringing you closer to the goal. Now I'm going to read the muslin and learn what it's telling me.

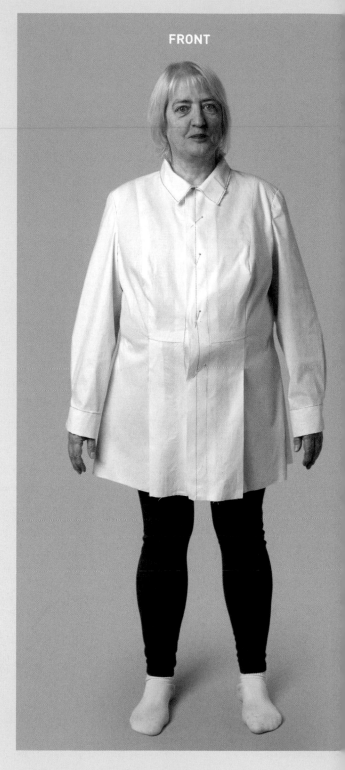

FRONT

FIRST FITTING: IDENTIFY THE WRINKLES

I discovered many of these same fitting issues when I studied Norma's candid wardrobe photos starting on p. 21. I will proceed in the same general order from neck and shoulders to anchor the muslin; then I'll work down the body, from chest to bust to waist to hem.

FRONT   When looking at Norma from the front in her original muslin, I can see the muslin shows vertical wrinkles across the chest and bust area, and the end of the shoulder sits too far down the arm. The horizontal wrinkles at the waist tell me there's too little fabric circumference there. The skirt hangs nicely below the waist.

RIGHT SIDE   Looking at Norma from the right, the garment shows horizontal wrinkles at the waist and pulls under the tummy. This indicates too little circumference in that area. I also can see that the collar sits too far away from the neck on the back, which indicates insufficient back length in the muslin. The sleeve hangs nicely, with enough wearing ease, but it needs to be shorter.

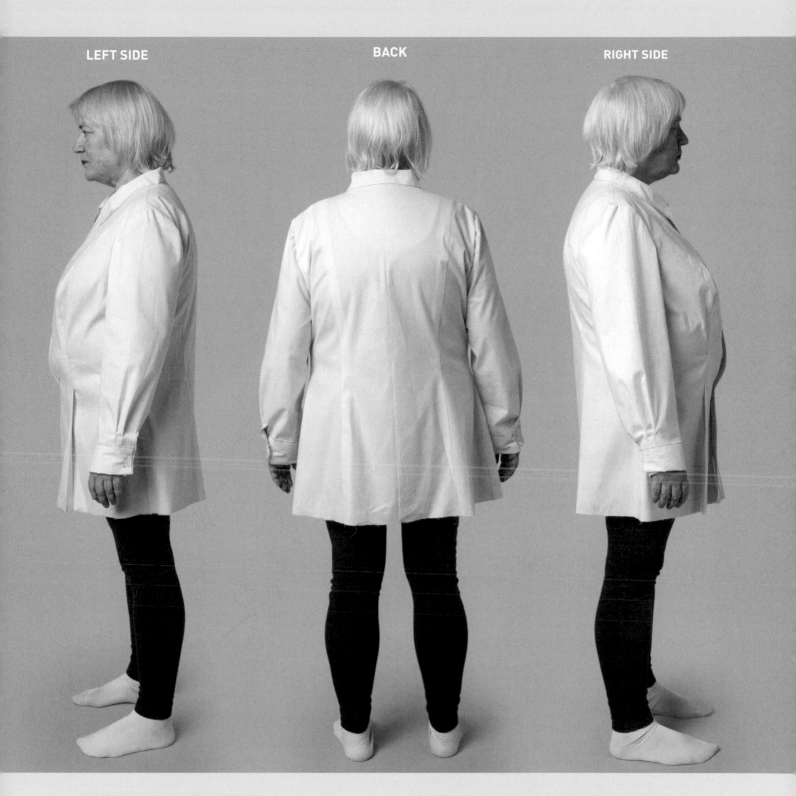

LEFT SIDE   The left side of the muslin tells much the same as the right side does. The horizontal wrinkles at the waist indicate insufficient circumference. The collar, again, sits too far from the neck, indicating insufficient back length in the muslin. The sleeve hangs nicely but also needs to be shorter.

BACK   From the back, diagonal wrinkles exist from the shoulder to the underarm. Diagonal wrinkles point from the waist area to the middle of the back in the shoulder blade area. These wrinkles indicate insufficient back length.

PIN OUT THE WRINKLES

NECK, SHOULDERS, AND TORSO

1. I first need to correct the shoulder width. I reduce width for a net loss by pinning out along the vertical princess seam, which solves the problem, as well as in the low armhole seam.

The alteration draws the armhole up into the proper position and corrects the shoulder width. It also reduces the sleeve length somewhat.

BUST

1. The vertical wrinkles in the bust area tell me to reduce the fabric there, a net loss. Pin along the princess lines until the wrinkle disappears to reduce the fabric there.

Upper-Body Circumference

If the body is broad across the back and narrow in the front, like Norma's, it raises concerns about the fit of the sleeve bicep. This is the case when you see wrinkles around the total circumference of the upper body—the arms as well as the upper chest. But if you make a significant net loss of fabric to allow the upper chest in front to fit smoothly with no ripples parallel to the armhole, you may inadvertently remove circumference and limit the lift on the sleeve.

In these cases, however, when you remove material across the upper chest in front to make it lie smoothly, you need to add it back to the sleeve bicep to make the total circumference around the upper body large enough for comfortable movement. In a sense, this is a no net change, since material is distributed across adjoining pieces of the garment.

WAISTLINE

1. Working down to the waist, I want the center front to hang perpendicular to the floor. To achieve this, I release the horizontal wrinkles by opening the side seam at the waist. I've chosen to open the seam on both sides to accurately assess how much circumference the muslin needs. Since there are wide seam allowances, this is easy to let out. If you didn't use a wide seam allowance, you will add muslin to fix the alteration.

Princess Seam Placement

Debates rage about the placement of princess lines that emerge from the shoulder seam. Some insist that they should cross over the bust apex. I learned to create, and find more appealing, a princess line that sits ½ in. to ¾ in. away from the apex toward the armhole. To my eye, this gives a more flattering appearance to the bust in relation to the waist.

BACK

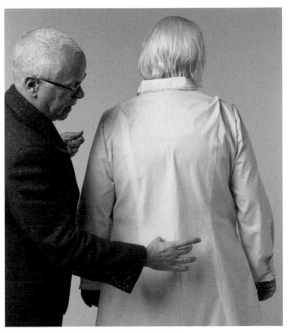

1. In the back shoulder blade area, notice the diagonal wrinkles toward the armholes and one vertical wrinkle at the center back. The muslin tells me two things there. First, the wrinkles near the armholes indicate the need to remove excess back width. This is a continuation of the pinning that was started on the front.

Second, the vertical wrinkle at the center back points to the need to increase the back length. Increasing this length will correct the center-back neckline so the collar sits properly at the base of Norma's neck.

PIN OUT THE WRINKLES

BACK WIDTH

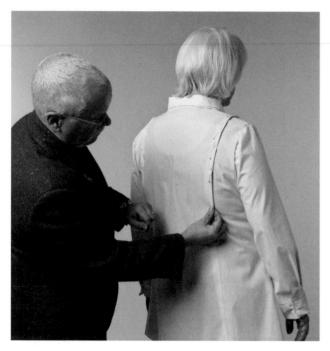

1. I will address the excess back width in the muslin before addressing the back length. Again, since this tunic has princess lines from the shoulder, I pin out the excess fabric along the princess lines, a net loss.

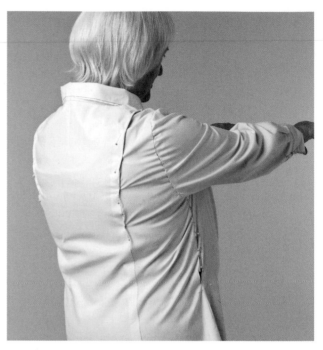

2. Before continuing, I have Norma check to see if the muslin gives her enough room to move. For this, I had her raise her arms. The fit is good.

Mobility Versus Appearance

Balance mobility and appearance based on the finished garment's eventual use. You sacrifice some appearance for more mobility. Norma's tunic is a casual garment, so more wearing ease is necessary for the daily activities of life, such as driving a car. There will be some wrinkling at the sides near the armholes to allow for this mobility.

If this were a more formal garment, you would want to smooth out more wrinkles in back. Although mobility would be diminished, if you can sit at a table and eat, dance with a partner, or close a car door, you have enough.

Back Length and Width Affect the Collar

The human body moves forward—we bend forward and we reach forward. This creates the need for more width across the back as well as more length down the back. Generally, back width is about 2 in. more than the front width when measured from armhole to armhole. Back length should be about 2 in. longer than the front length from the base of the neck to the waist.

Both insufficient back width and insufficient back length can cause the collar to pull away from the base of the neck in back.

If, as in Norma's case, you seat the collar at the base of the neck, you get what I call the "shark fin"—a vertical wrinkle that points toward the base of the neck. You can see this in the photo below.

This wrinkle tells me there is insufficient back length. When I pull the lower edge of the garment down so the wrinkle disappears, I then measure the distance from the base of the neck to the center back of the neck seam on the garment. This provides the amount to add, which is a net gain.

If, however, there isn't a shark fin when you seat the collar at the base of the neck, but the collar still pulls away from the neck while wearing the garment, the muslin says to add back width. This will be a net gain.

After pulling the muslin down at the hem so the vertical wrinkle disappears, you can see that the back length is too short to reach the base of Norma's neck. Measure the distance from the collar seam to the base of the neck. This is how I determine how much back length to add.

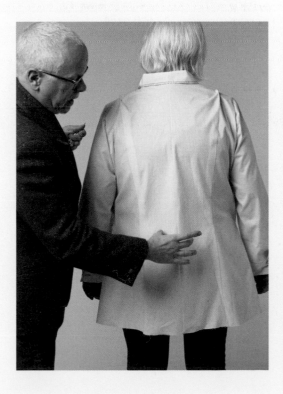

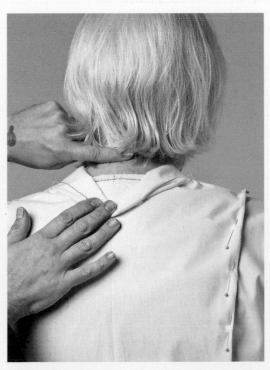

PIN OUT THE WRINKLES

BACK LENGTH

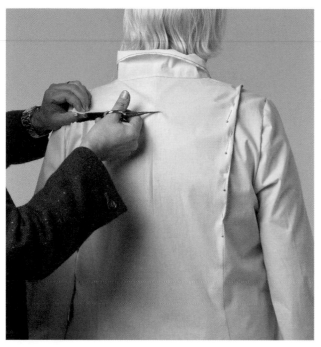

1. Adding back length, which occurs in two steps, creates a net gain. First, slash the muslin across the shoulder blades, from armhole to armhole. This cut doesn't have to be dead parallel to the floor, just approximate.

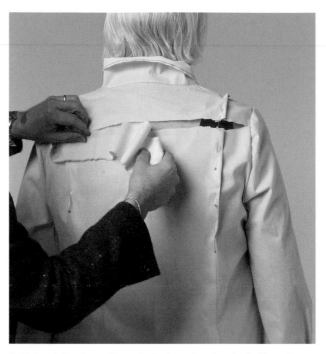

2. Cut a strip of muslin and slip it under the slash. Seat the collar at the true base of the neck; then pin the top edge of the slash to the muslin strip.

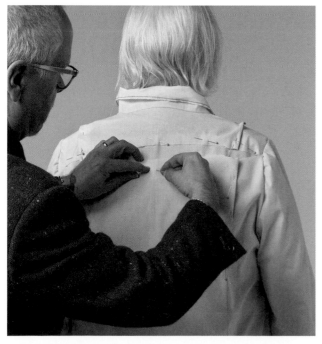

3. Pull the lower portion of the garment down so it hangs smoothly. When you're satisfied the garment hangs nicely over the shoulders, pin the lower edge of the slash to the strip. This "fixes" the alteration.

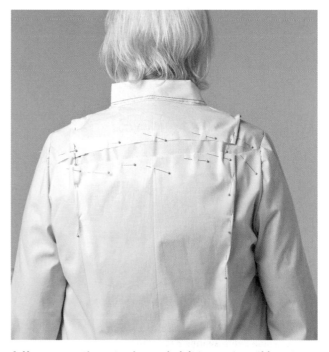

4. You can see the net gain needed. It tapers to nothing at the armholes.

GARMENT SWINGS FORWARD

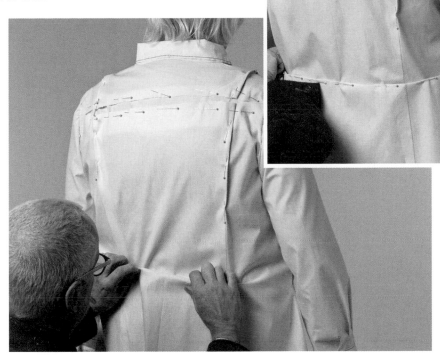

1. Notice how the garment swings forward. This indicates that another adjustment to the back needs to be made.

2. I added fabric to the upper back to accommodate the curve there, but now I need to remove fabric from the lower back below the waist to correct the hang of the garment. Norma is longer above her waist than the pattern is.

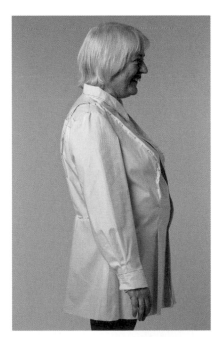

3. Pin the excess length at the waist until the side seam swings back into the proper position. Adding to the upper back and removing from the lower back creates a no net change.

TIP // WE SEE HERE THAT CORRECTING ONE ISSUE (THE COLLAR SITS PROPERLY AT THE NECK) CAUSES ANOTHER ISSUE (THE GARMENT SWINGS FORWARD). DON'T DESPAIR! THIS IS THE BEAUTY OF UNDERSTANDING NO NET CHANGE. LOOK FOR IT WHEN YOU'RE FITTING—IT EXPLAINS MANY OTHERWISE UNEXPECTED OUTCOMES.

PIN OUT THE WRINKLES

WAIST

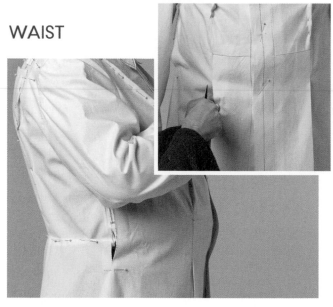

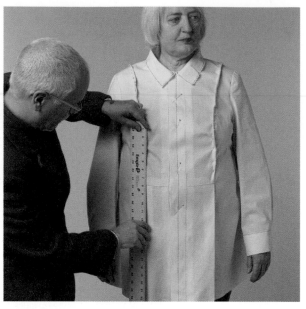

1. Looking at the muslin from the side, I can see a pull just below the waist. This says the pleat, which is stitched down, needs to be released—and this will make the garment more flattering. Just because the pattern has a detail doesn't mean you must use it. I release the pleat stitching on both sides.

2. To finish the waist, I check to see if the horizontal seam at the waist is level with the floor. Be sure to check both sides. Also check the hem to see if it's horizontal. A little variation (under 1 in.) can be corrected when hemming the final garment. If there is more variation than that, repin to accommodate the excess.

SLEEVES

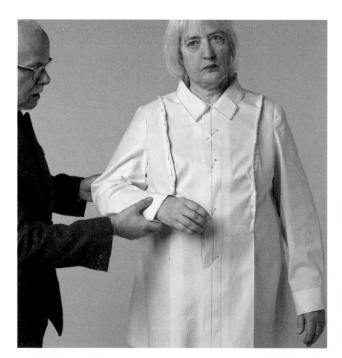

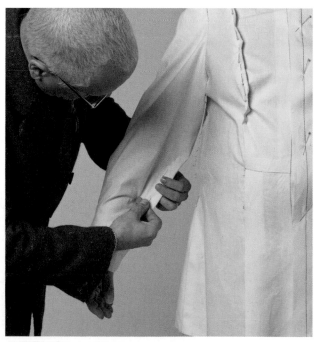

1. The final alteration is to the sleeve. Ideally, the sleeve length should sit at the dip in front of the prominent bone in the wrist when the elbow is bent at 90 degrees.

2. Although the sleeve length is good, there's too much fabric across the elbow. This is a personal preference. Pin out whatever amount of circumference you want to remove from the sleeve to create the most flattering line.

THE PINNED-OUT MUSLIN

Norma's muslin requires a decent amount of alteration, so I likely will need to refine the fit in the next muslin. First, though, I will transfer the changes to the pattern.

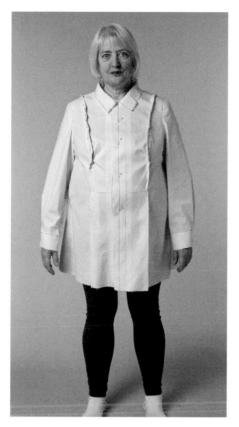

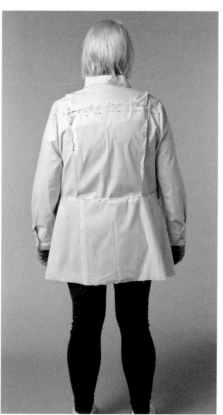

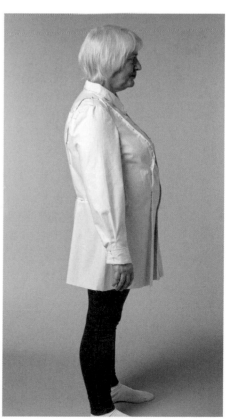

SARAH

Sarah chose a dress pattern with vertical seams, bracelet-length sleeves, and a rice bowl neckline. I adjusted her shoulder slope and lengths to some degree during the muslin construction based on her measurements. Now, let's see what the wrinkles say.

FIRST FITTING: IDENTIFY THE WRINKLES

FRONT The top of the armhole seam sits past the actual shoulder. However, looking at the pattern, I read the shoulder seam placement as intentional to the design.

The shoulder slope needs to be lowered near the neck seam. Vertical wrinkles near the armhole tell me that there's too much fabric across the upper chest area. Horizontal wrinkles across the bust tell me that more fabric should be added in this area. Ripples directly under the bust and the wave on the skirt front may fall out once the corrections to the upper body are made.

BACK From the back, the prominent wrinkles are horizontal and diagonal. These indicate two different issues. The horizontal wrinkles, combined with the hem rising in front, indicate there is too much length for the curve at the small of the back along the center back, which needs to be folded out. The diagonal wrinkle traveling from the right waist to the left side seam indicates a twist. Letting the left seam out will correct this by adding more fabric to that seam.

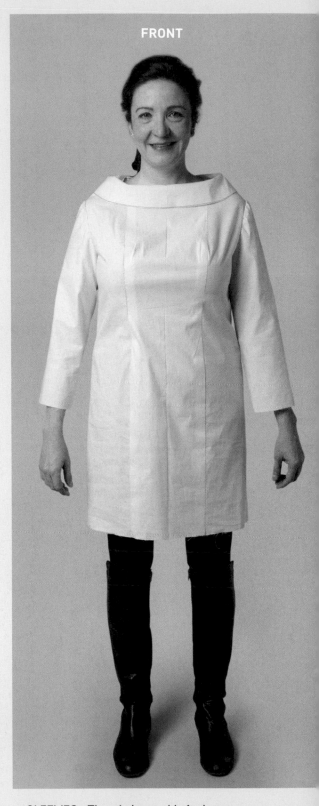

FRONT

SLEEVES The right and left sleeves have similar problems by degrees. This is clear in the sleeve photos, but it also can be seen from the back photo. The right shoulder is turned significantly forward.

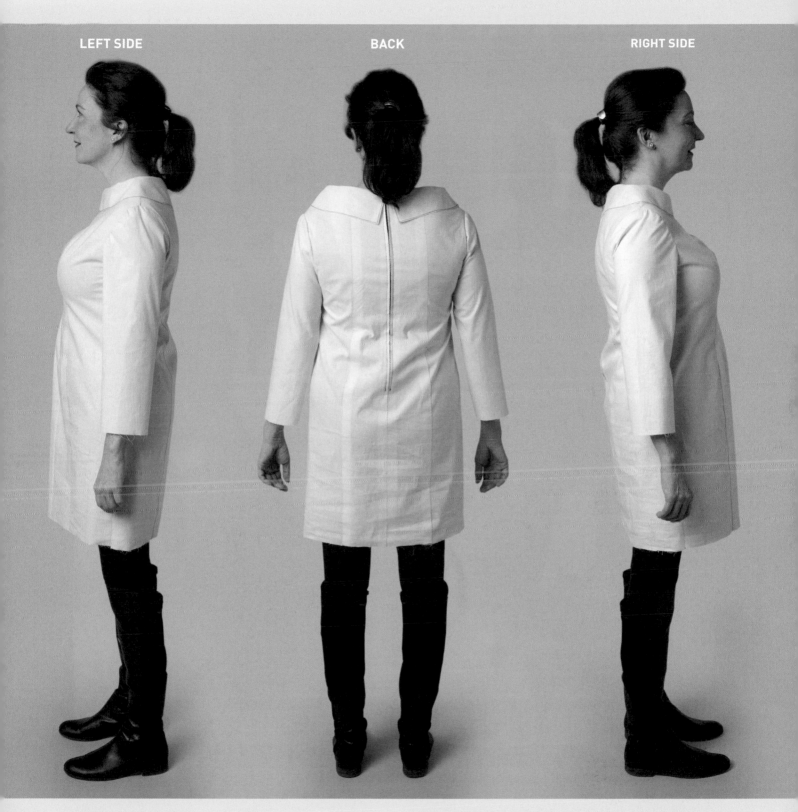

RIGHT SIDE   Diagonal drag lines on the upper sleeve cap point toward the front, indicating that a redistribution of ease is needed on the cap. Note that the pitch of the sleeve is correct, however. These alterations are a no net change because no fabric is subtracted or added.

LEFT SIDE   From the left, the sleeve cap looks smoother than the right sleeve, as the ease is more evenly distributed. Even though adjusting the sleeves is the same process, it is not to the same degree because one needs more correction than the other.

PIN OUT THE WRINKLES

SHOULDER SLOPE

1. Beginning at the shoulders, I pin out the excess on both front and back, starting at the neck seam and tapering toward the armhole. This correction will extend up onto the collar as well.

2. I correct both sides to anchor the dress securely.

TIP // AS COCO CHANEL SAID, "THE SHOULDERS WEAR THE DRESS." HOWEVER YOU SAY IT, THE MEANING IS THE SAME: GETTING A GOOD SHOULDER FIT IS IMPORTANT BECAUSE THE PROPER FIT ANCHORS THE GARMENT.

UPPER CHEST

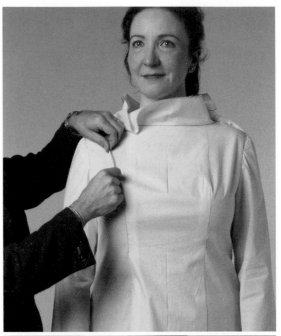

1. Remember, you want to work down the front of a garment when pinning out, looking for the next wrinkles to pin. On Sarah's muslin, the vertical wrinkles between the armhole and the princess seam tell me I need to remove fabric there, a net loss. Pin first one side of the body, then the other.

BACK

1. Fitting from the top down can result in fixing wrinkles elsewhere before you get to pinning them. This is just what happened at the back waist on Sarah's muslin—some of the wrinkles indicating a twist at the waist have disappeared.

BUST

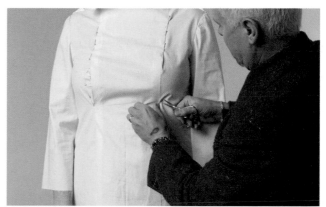

1. The horizontal wrinkles at and below the bust tell us that more fabric is needed across this area. Open the vertical seams over the bust. This is a net gain.

2. Repin the princess seams, adding in a scrap of fabric if it's needed.

NOTE: Wide seam allowances come in handy for fixing the princess seams. Here I split the difference, adding some width to the front panel and some to the side panel.

PIN OUT THE WRINKLES

BUST (CONTINUED)

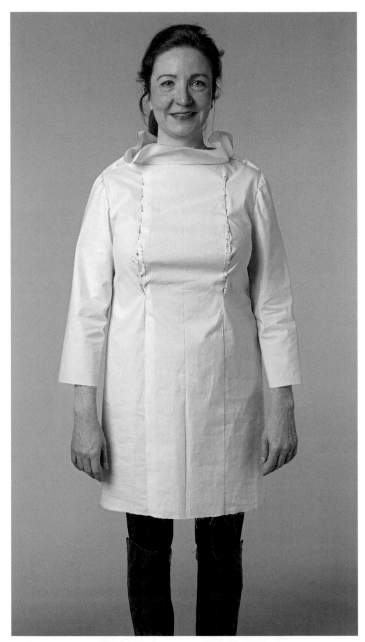

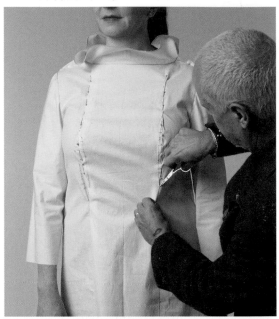

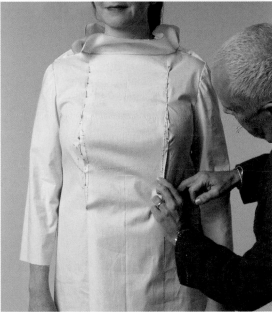

3. There is still a horizontal wrinkle under the bust. This tells me to add more fabric across the midriff.

4. Open the princess seams below the bust. Let out the seams across the midriff, below the pinned bust area; then repin the princess seams, adding the needed fabric.

Where to Position Princess Seams

Generally, you make a width alteration to the side panel, but in this case, I add to both the front and side panels. The position of the princess lines will tell you how to make the alteration. In this case, the princess lines appear to be too close together. But if all of the width was added to just the front panel, then the lines would appear to be too far apart. Adding width across both panels gives a more flattering appearance to the garment.

When adding width to both panels, you will likely repin the seams a couple of times to ensure that the position of the seams looks good.

SIDE

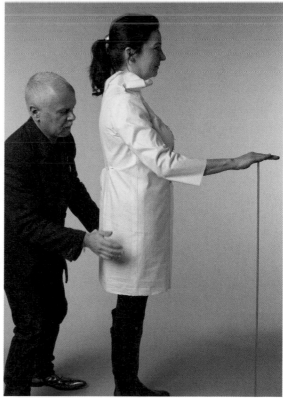

1. The side seam in the muslin swings toward the front, and the horizontal wrinkle across the small of the back needs to be eliminated. These two combined conditions tell me there's too much length across the small of the back, requiring a net loss.

PIN OUT THE WRINKLES

SIDE (CONTINUED)

2. Pick up the skirt at the center-back waist, and fold out the excess muslin, tapering to nothing at the side seams. This is an easy alteration because of the princess-line style.

Once the correction has been made, you can see that the side seam hangs perpendicular to the floor.

3. There is still the shadow of a diagonal wrinkle extending from the right waist to the left hip, indicating the muslin needs extra fabric along the left skirt side seam. In this photo, the muslin is twisting on the left side, and the fabric in that area needs to be adjusted for the asymmetry of Sarah's hips.

The seam on the left side also appears to sit too far back. I decided to open the seam and add fabric to the back, to reposition the seam and eliminate the diagonal wrinkle.

 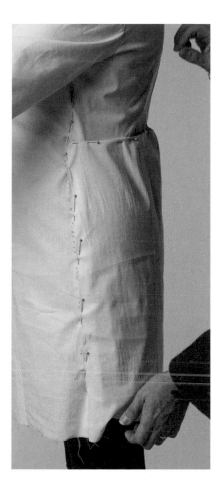 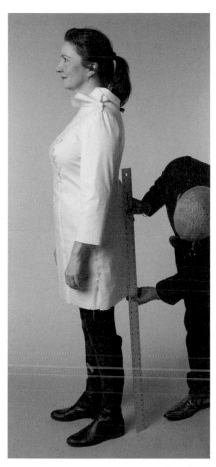

4. This is a net gain, since the alteration is being made to the left skirt back only. Open the seam up to the waist and repin, adding to the back by letting out the seam allowance.

5. This detail shows the side seam hanging correctly. You can see how this alteration merges with the adjustment made across the back. I kept inching out the back seam until the skirt was smooth; then I pinned it out.

6. As a check, I measure up from the floor to the hem to make sure the hem is level. It is.

PIN OUT THE WRINKLES

BACK SHOULDERS

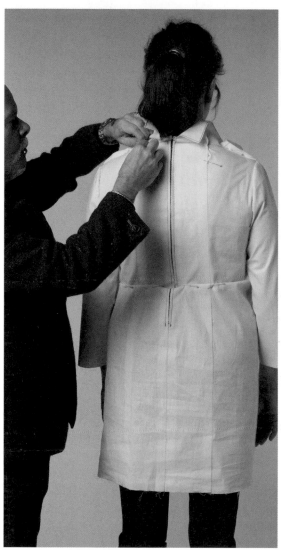

1. One more check on the back shows some slight vertical wrinkles near the neck seam under the collar, along the princess seams. This tells me I need to pin out the excess along the princess seams so the neckline sits smoothly against the back. This correction extends up onto the collar as well.

SLEEVE

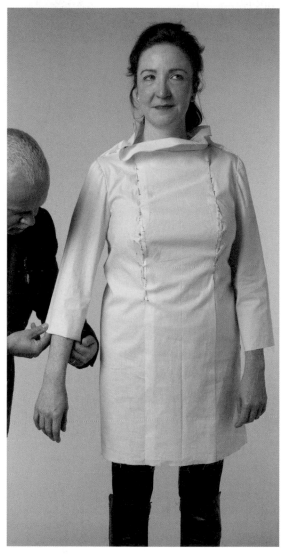

1. After fitting the body, I check the sleeve for adequate bicep ease, mobility, and proper length. There's plenty of bicep ease, and the arm can be raised to a 45-degree angle, which is adequate for dresses. Since this is a bracelet-length sleeve, the length is variable and dependent on the wearer. Sarah and I decided on a proper length, and I pinned.

THE PINNED-OUT MUSLIN

You can see the fit difference in Sarah's dress once the muslin is pinned out. It's time to make alterations to the pattern based on the muslin adjustments.

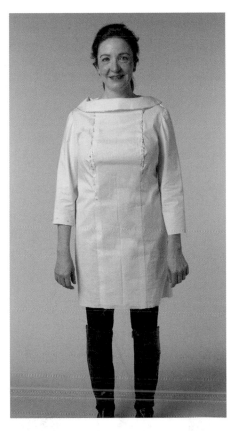

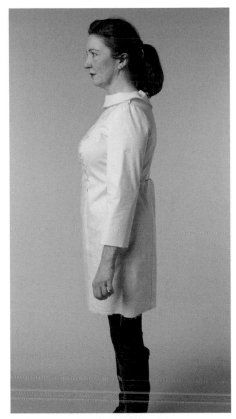

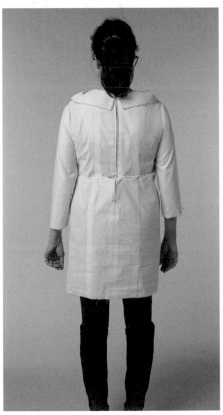

ROSANN

Rosann's chosen dress pattern has three vertical seams across the front and back and a slit jewel neckline. It can be sewn with or without sleeves. Rosann wants the option of making the dress either way. In this case, it's wise to get the bodice fitting properly before adding the sleeve. In this way, issues that might show up in the sleeve are easier to address because we are dealing with a corrected armhole. When you do add the sleeve, I recommend hand basting it into the bodice. It makes taking off the sleeves easier.

Remember the sneak peek we had when studying the candid photos of Rosann in her own clothes in Part I? That was a preview of the fitting issues that will be addressed here. Now, let's read what the muslin is saying about this garment.

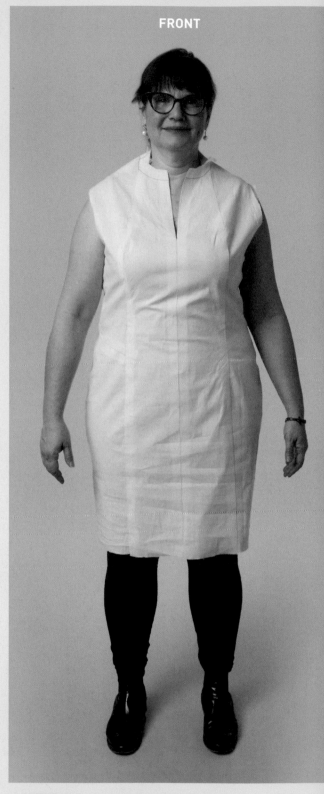

FRONT

FIRST FITTING: IDENTIFY THE WRINKLES

FRONT First, study the muslin from the front. The shoulder slopes need adjustment, which will eventually correct some of the wrinkles farther down on the dress. Also, there are wrinkles emanating from the bust toward the armholes and angling down toward the hip (you can see this in the right side view), indicating excess fabric across the chest area. These are created by the combination of the incorrect shoulder slope and the excess we need to fold out at the armhole. This is a net loss adjustment.

LEFT SIDE Rosann's left side looks much the same as her right; she is fairly symmetrical. Except for the shoulder slope, the wrinkles on the left side indicate what is showing on the right.

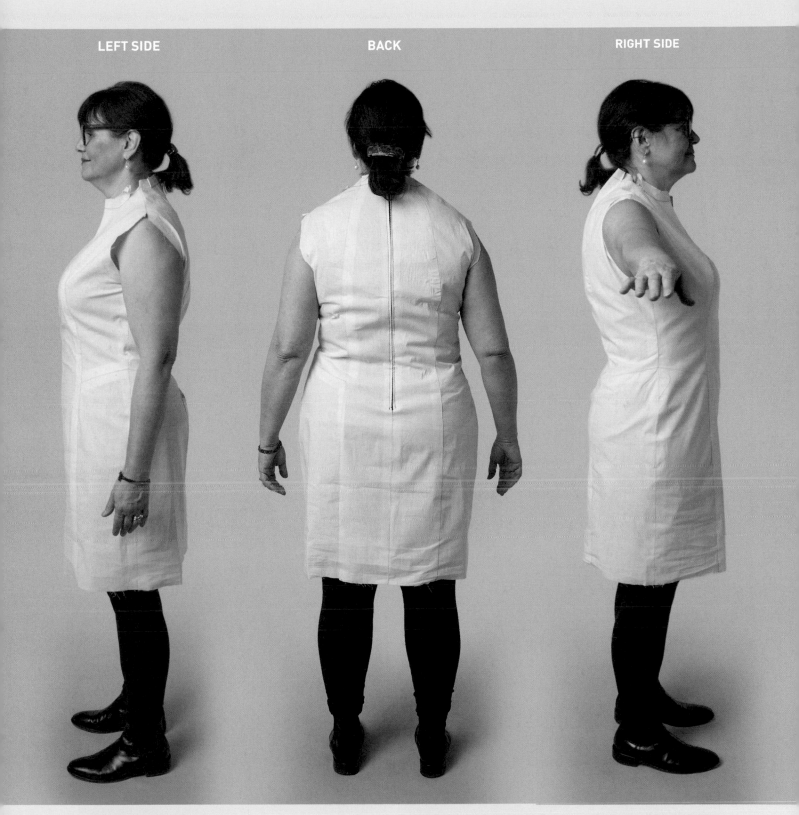

RIGHT SIDE   From the right side, notice the diagonal wrinkles from the bust, traveling under Rosann's arm toward her hips in back. I can see a wrinkle at the armhole, which needs fixing. This is a net loss of fabric, which will reduce the armhole circumference. The muslin neckline sits properly at the base of Rosann's neck.

BACK   Looking at Rosann from the back, I see the proper shoulder slope and neck placement. The horizontal wrinkles in the waist area are further indication that the muslin doesn't have sufficient circumference around the lower torso.

PIN OUT THE WRINKLES

NECK AND SHOULDERS

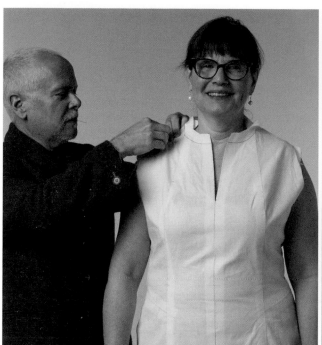

1. The position of the shoulder slope makes the entire bodice slightly too long. Rosann's shoulders don't slope as much as the garment's. And one shoulder is higher than the other. I pin the shoulder seam in at the neck base to make the garment hang better. The neckline is what indicates the need to make this alteration—it doesn't hang smoothly but bows in slightly toward the body, indicating too much fabric.

2. Rosann's right shoulder is lower than her left, so I pin them differently. The wrinkle on the left shoulder tells me to let that shoulder out slightly, which will release the wrinkle, a net gain. Repin the left shoulder.

FRONT PRINCESS SEAM

1. With the vertical wrinkle at the shoulder gone, I need to address the wrinkle going from the armhole to the bust. This is caused by too much fabric in this area and will be a net loss.

2. Pin out this excess muslin on both sides, tapering to nothing at the princess seam. This will be a net loss, folded out in the pattern.

3. Vertical wrinkles between the princess seam and the armhole tell us there is excess width across the chest. Removing this excess fabric is easy. Just open the top of the princess seam and fit the excess from the side panel into the seam for a net loss.

PIN OUT THE WRINKLES

WAIST AND HIPS

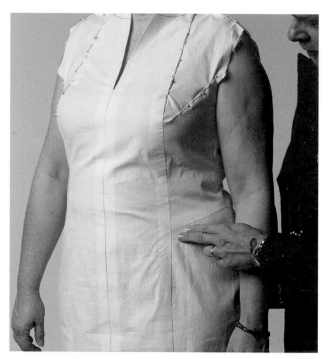

1. With the bodice corrected, I move down to the waist and hip area, where I can see horizontal wrinkles in the muslin across the abdomen just below the waist. This indicates that there is too little circumference across the front of the muslin.

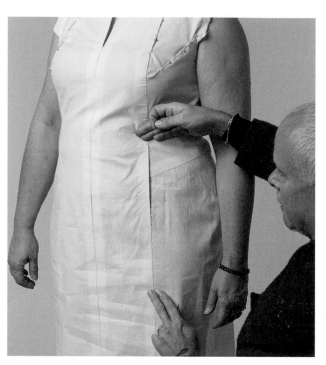

2. Open the seam in the area from the upper thigh to the waist—the fabric automatically spreads to indicate the amount you need to add for a net gain.

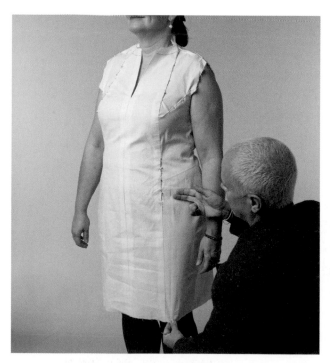

3. Repin the seam into the new position.

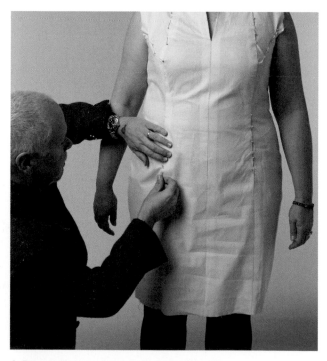

4. Repeat the process for the opposite side.

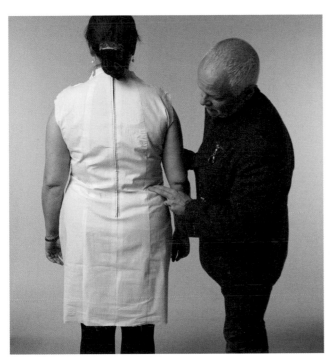

5. Looking at the muslin back, I see horizontal wrinkles at the small of the back. We saw this symptom on Sarah when the back was too long because Sarah has very erect posture. Folding out the excess back length resulted in a net loss. In Rosann's case, the cause for the wrinkles is too little circumference across the hips, which causes the garment to ride up and bunch at the small of the back. The cause of the problem determines the fix, which in Rosann's case is the lack of circumference at the hips.

You may have to pin out both corrections to see which one solves the problem correctly. For example, when I fold out the excess back length, I see the side seam swings farther to the back. This tells me the problem isn't an incorrect back length but rather insufficient width across the hips. If you aren't sure which problem you have, compare the fit and solution shown here with a similar issue that shortens the back length for Sarah (see pp. 99–101).

A Net Loss Approach to Smoothing Out a Skirt

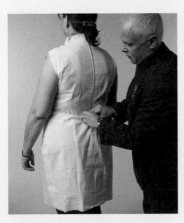

1. Fold out the excess, starting at the center back and working toward the side seams; taper to zero at the side seams.

2. Smooth out the skirt to see how it hangs.

3. Once the skirt is smoothed out, I can clearly see that the side seam below the waist swings toward the back, which is not what I intended. This indicates that I need to let the garment out at the hips instead of folding out at the waist.

WAIST AND HIPS (CONTINUED)

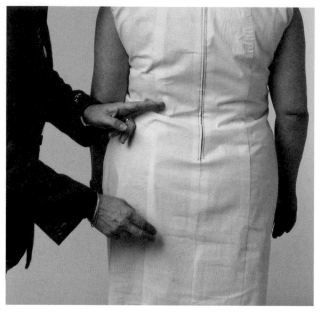

6. The diagonal lines we saw in the side views of the muslin indicated that there wasn't enough fabric across the hips in back. I will add fabric for a net gain.

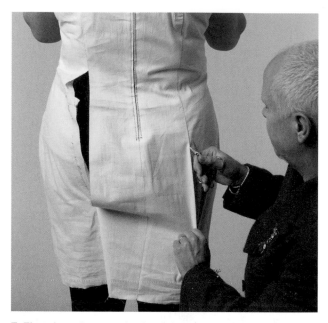

7. First, I need to open both princess seams from the hem to about 2 in. above the waist. I didn't initially cut all the way down to the hem but left the seams attached to control the two sides. (After I pinned out the muslin, I continued opening the seam to the hem.) Next, I cut strips of muslin about 4 in. wide and 18 in. long.

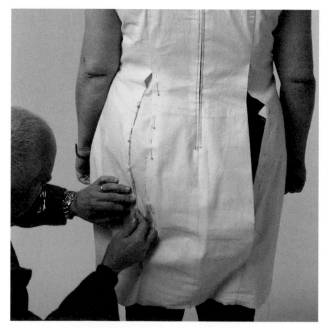

8. Working on one side at a time, I pin the muslin strip first to the center-panel princess seam. I smooth out the muslin and pin the princess side panel to the strip, creating the amount of net gain needed in that area. The process is repeated on the opposite princess seamline.

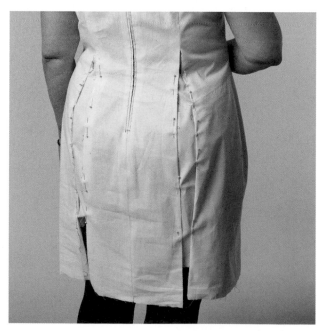

9. Check to see that both inserted pieces are symmetrical. The wrinkle at the waist disappears.

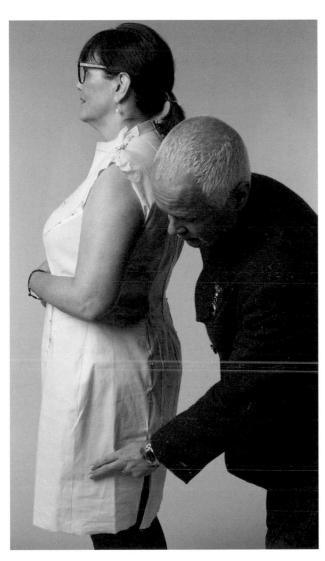

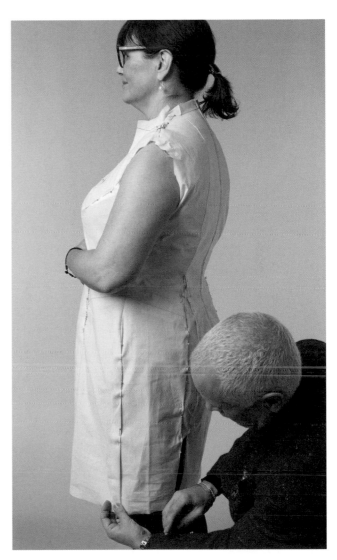

10. Check the side seam again. It now hangs perpendicular to the floor, but it sits too far forward. Also, the vertical wrinkle indicates there is extra fullness in the hips at the sides.

11. Pin out the extra fullness by overlapping the front over the back. The net loss occurs on the back of the skirt only, and the seam sits perpendicular to the floor.

This seam now angles ever so slightly toward the front, but for a first muslin with so many corrections, I've decided to wait and check it and adjust it, if needed, in the second muslin. The problem might disappear in the corrections.

PIN OUT THE WRINKLES

SLEEVES

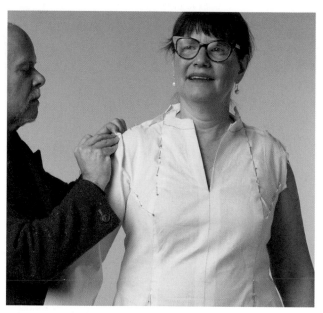

1. Now that the dress is fitted, I can set the sleeve. Turn the sleeve cap seam allowances under on the seamline and slide the sleeve onto the arm. Align the shoulder match point and pin at the top of the sleeve cap.

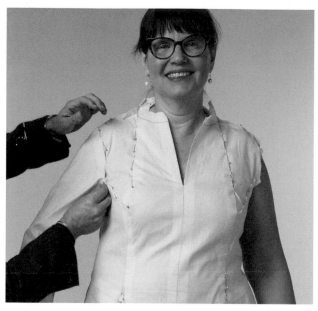

2. Check to see that the sleeve hangs smoothly, with no diagonal wrinkles on the cap. Diagonal wrinkles indicate that the sleeve is at an incorrect pitch. Adjust as needed by rotating it slightly forward or backward. Once you are sure the sleeve hangs smoothly, pin the rest of it into the armhole.

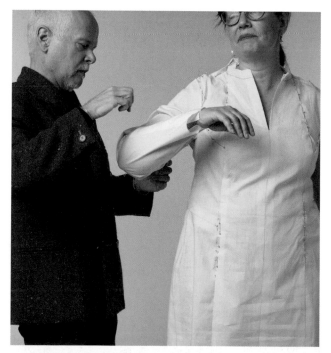

3. Check the sleeve for mobility. When fitting a dress or jacket, I aim for the ability to raise the arm at a 45-degree angle to the body without binding at the bicep. For a long sleeve, the cuff generally sits at the prominent bone on the wrist when the arm is bent at a 90-degree angle.

TIP // THERE'S A LITTLE MEMORY TRICK I USE WHEN EVALUATING FIT ON A SLEEVE ONCE IT HAS BEEN INSTALLED INTO THE MUSLIN. WHEN WRINKLES START LOW IN THE BACK BICEP AND POINT DIAGONALLY TOWARD THE FRONT SHOULDER, THE SLEEVE SHOULD BE SHIFTED FRONTWARD. IF THE SITUATION IS REVERSED, AND THE WRINKLES START LOWER ON THE FRONT BICEP AND POINT UP TOWARD THE BACK, THE SLEEVE NEEDS SHIFTING TO THE BACK. THIS REPRESENTS A NO NET CHANGE OF SORTS, AS YOU AREN'T ADDING OR SUBTRACTING FABRIC BUT REARRANGING IT.

THE PINNED-OUT MUSLIN

Here is the pinned muslin. Because Rosann's arms are symmetrical, I only needed to pin out one sleeve. You may get a little bit of vertical wrinkling pointing to the sleeve cap, but fixing this is a judgment call of mobility versus appearance. The vertical wrinkles parallel to the armhole add range of motion. For this first muslin, I will keep them and revisit the appearance after the major corrections have been made.

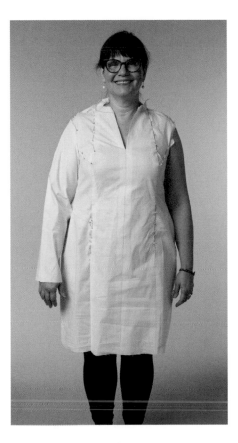
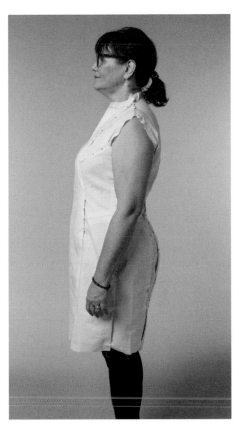
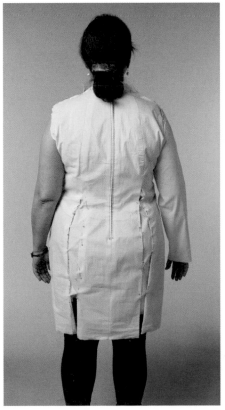

JEANNINE

Jeannine's dress pattern has several design details that add elegant style to a garment. The shoulder yoke opens the V-shaped front neckline, which is framed by a fabric insert, as shown in the photo below. These design elements have figure-flattering elements as well: The gathers over the bust can suit both a slight and full bust; the vertical lines of the pleats are slenderizing for

most bodies and keep the upper part of the skirt close to the body. The dress closes with an underarm side-seam zipper.

FRONT

FIRST FITTING: IDENTIFY THE WRINKLES

FRONT From the front, the wrinkles on Jeannine's right side, under her arm, tell me to lower the shoulder on that side. Also, I see the sleeve is too long and needs to be shortened.

RIGHT SIDE Jeannine's right side shows the wrinkles under her arm. The diagonal wrinkles on the sleeve pointing toward the front normally indicate a need for adjustment, but I will assess the sleeve after picking up the shoulder to see if further action is needed. The hem is level with the floor, so there's nothing to address there.

LEFT SIDE The left and right sides are very similar.

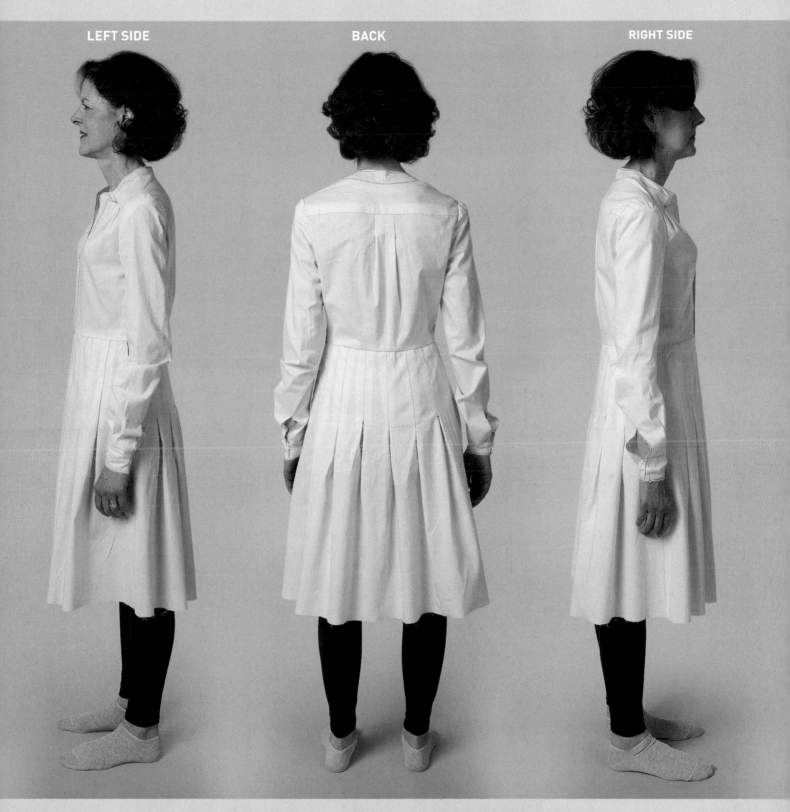

LEFT SIDE

BACK

RIGHT SIDE

BACK   From the back, the fabric appears to collapse in areas, which indicates the bodice could be lifted at the shoulders a bit. While the muslin fits well, there is a little too much circumference at the waist. Jeannine is slender, and the dress will benefit from being taken in at the waist.

PIN OUT THE WRINKLES

NECK AND SHOULDERS

1. To smooth out the wrinkles under the right arm, pick up the muslin at the shoulder to remove excess fabric there. This tapers to zero at the armhole and is a net loss.

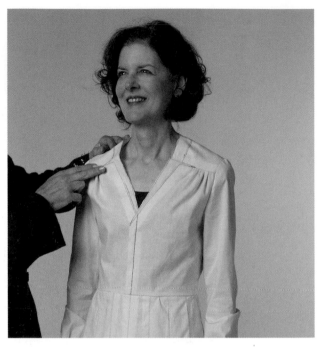

2. Adjusting the shoulder affects the neckline, which shows some gapping. This requires a net loss to make the neckline sit flat against the chest.

Gapping in V Necklines

When drafting a V neckline, automatically lower the top of the V by ¼ in. at the front bodice shoulder only and redraft the shoulder. This will remove the gap. Don't assume that the neckline gap has been taken into account in a commercial pattern, because it may not have been. Your first muslin will let you know.

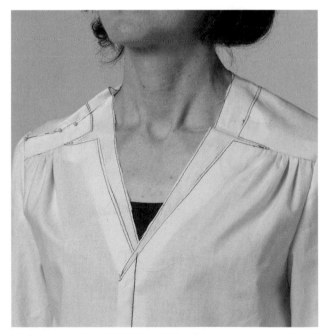

3. Once this net loss is pinned out, the neckline sits flat against the chest. Notice I've pinned this out in the yoke section only. Pinning on the yoke won't disturb the seaming detail where the yoke joins the band and bodice.

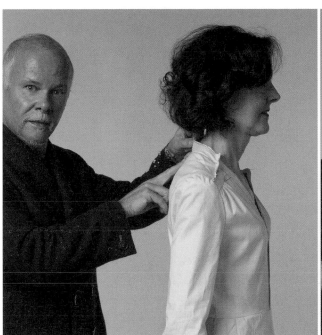

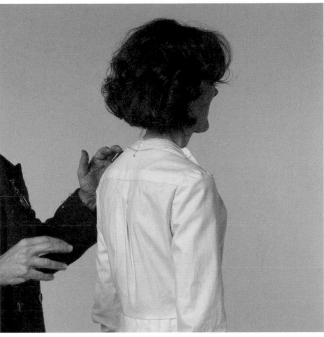

4. Working around the muslin, you can see that the back neckline stands slightly away from the center-back neck. This requires a net loss as well. I pin this out, tapering to the yoke seam, which represents a net loss in the pattern.

5. To make the gathers on the left side of the bodice hang more smoothly and to make the neckline at the shoulder lie flat, I need to lift the left shoulder. This fold tapers to zero at the armhole. If you recall, this is the same adjustment we made to the right shoulder, but the amounts differ. The result is a net loss in the pattern.

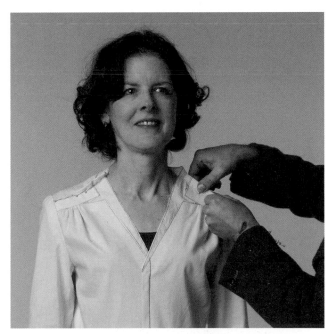

6. Pin out the net loss so that both sides hang nicely. The object is for the garment to look good on the body. If the body is asymmetrical, the sides won't necessarily be even.

PIN OUT THE WRINKLES

WAIST

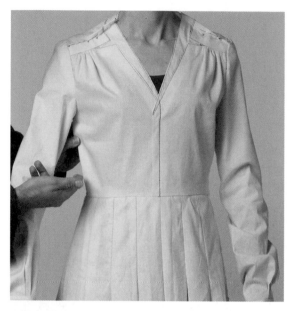

1. Visually, the bodice appears to be the same width from the shoulders down to the waist, and because Jeannine has a small waist, there is excess fabric here. I remove the excess at the right side seam to create negative space between the torso and arm, which is more flattering.

I didn't alter the left side because the zipper is set into that seam, but the pattern work will reflect the alteration on both sides later.

2. Pin out the excess at the waist, which represents a net loss.

SLEEVES

1. As I've said before, the cuff of the sleeve should sit in the dip between the hand and the prominent bone on the wrist. Clearly, these sleeves are too long for Jeannine's arms. I will pin out the excess length on the sleeves for a net loss.

TIP // FITTING THE CUFF IS A PERSONAL PREFERENCE. SOME LIKE THE CUFF TIGHTER; SOME LIKE IT LOOSER. THE MINIMUM WEARING EASE FOR A CUFF IS 1 IN. TO 1¼ IN.

THE PINNED-OUT MUSLIN

Jeannine's pinned muslin fits her slender frame and provides the right amount of wearing ease. It now goes to the cutting table to be marked, disassembled, and used to transfer the fitting information to the original pattern, which you can see in Part III.

EVAMARIE

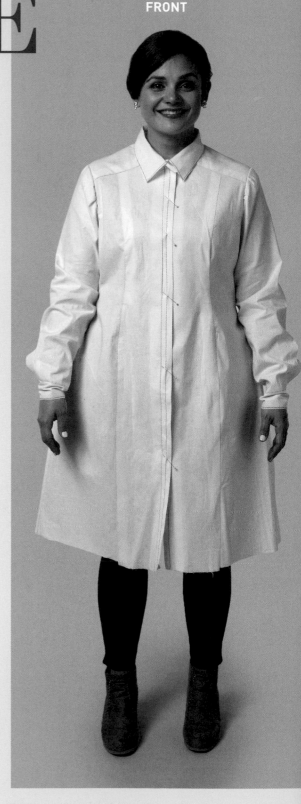

Evamarie's pattern is a coat-style dress that buttons up the front, with a shoulder yoke, collar, and collar band; long, cuffed sleeves; and vertical seams from the hem to the yoke on the front and back. Three dresses in this pattern collection have vertical seams, but not all vertical seams are princess seams. Whatever these are called, they offer a wonderful advantage for getting a good fit because they provide another location to expand or reduce the garment at a seam.

When I prepared the pattern for Evamarie, I appreciated the advantages of multisize patterns. Evamarie is different sizes from top to bottom, and the multisize pattern enabled me to match her actual measurements for bust, waist, and hips to the different patterns.

FIRST FITTING: IDENTIFY THE WRINKLES

FRONT Looking at Evamarie from the front, I see too much fabric across the upper chest area. The waist area also shows too much fabric that disguises Evamarie's waist. The sleeves are too long.

RIGHT SIDE On the right side, there is too much fabric across the front in the midriff area under the bust due to the diagonal wrinkles that travel from the bust to under the arms to the back. The hem is lower in the back than in the front.

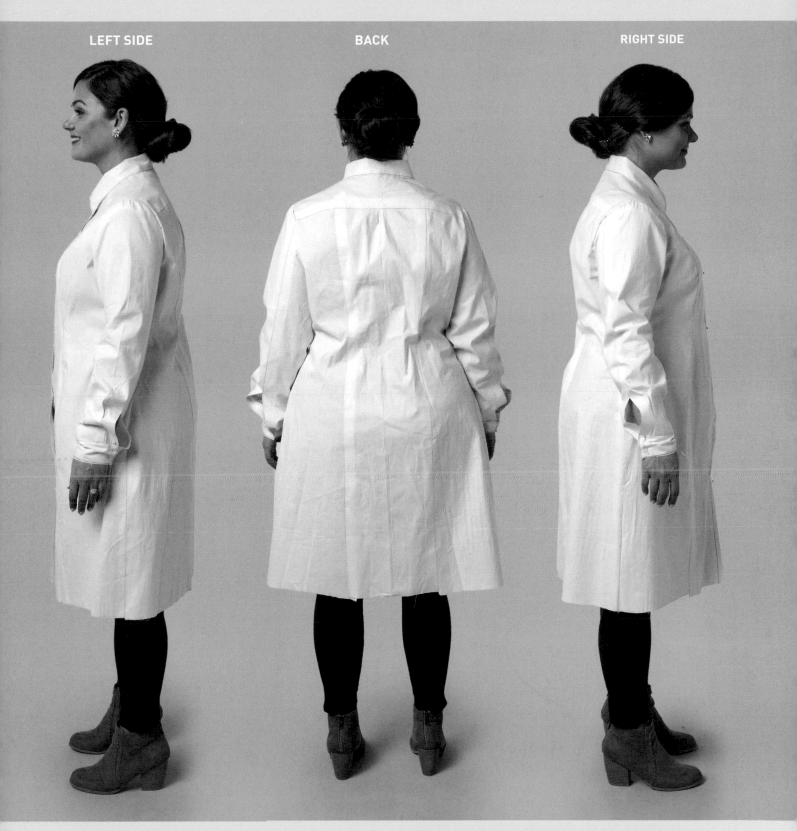

LEFT SIDE   The left side looks much like the right side, as Evamarie is symmetrical.

BACK   From the back, the muslin seems to have adequate wearing ease across the shoulder blade area and at the hips. The ripples at the small of the back indicate too much length and the need for a correction.

PIN OUT THE WRINKLES

NECK AND SHOULDERS

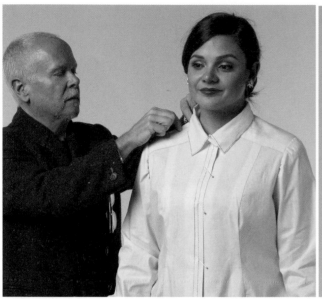

1. As mentioned previously, start pinning from the shoulders down. I need to refine the shoulders on Evamarie's dress with a slight net loss to make it sit better against the neck. The photos on p. 42 show what net loss looks like before pinning and after pinning.

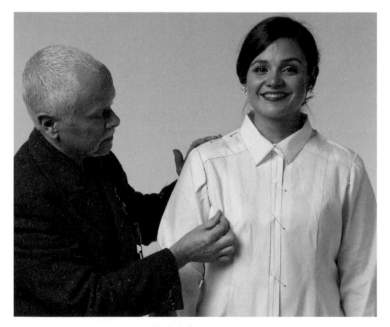
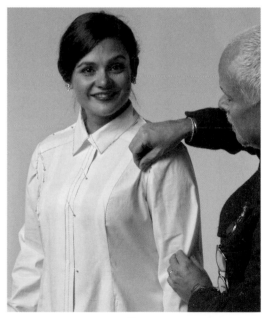

2. To remove the excess fabric across the upper chest area, pin out the vertical wrinkle as a net loss.

You can either pin this alteration directly along the vertical seam and remove the excess there, or pin the reduction between seams and use the grid to transfer the correction back to the seam. I've chosen to take this as a grid alteration (pinning out a double-ended dart), because the wrinkle sits midway between the armhole and vertical seam. The correction still transfers to the vertical seam, but for my demonstration purposes, I am showing this as a grid. It works both ways.

3. For balance, I'll make the same alteration to the other side.

BACK WAIST

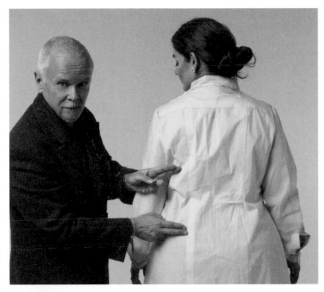

1. Working down to the waist, the back alteration is made first.

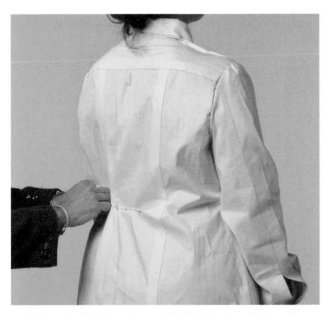

2. Pick up the fabric at the small of the back, and pin out the excess fabric to form a horizontal fold at the natural waistline. By removing the excess fabric, the wrinkles relax above the waist. Work from one side to the other across the back. This alteration is pinned the same as a previous waist alteration, but the pattern adjustment differs.

3. After pinning the waist, the side seam angles back slightly, which tells me the waist alteration will result as a no net change. This alteration also changes the location of the hip, lifting it to match Evamarie's figure.

If the side seam angled forward before the alteration and then fell plumb to the floor after folding out at the waist, this would be a net loss alteration because compensation is necessary at the hem.

PIN OUT THE WRINKLES

BODICE

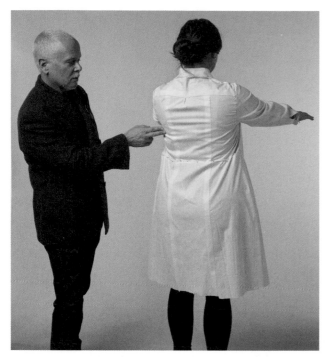

1. To check the bodice wearing ease, I have Evamarie raise her arms to see if this dress is comfortable for daily activities. It is.

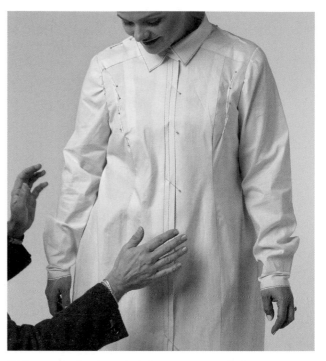

2. The center front needs to hang square, so before adjusting the front, I match the center-front lines and pin the center opening closed.

3. When I look at the muslin from the side, I can see that it sits too far away from the figure below the bust, which means there's too much fabric across the front. I follow the customary way to remove fabric in a princess line alteration and take it from the side panel. It's best to make the alteration on both right and left sides, giving more shape to the muslin and showing Evamarie's figure to best advantage.

MIDRIFF

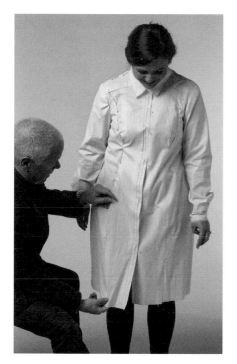 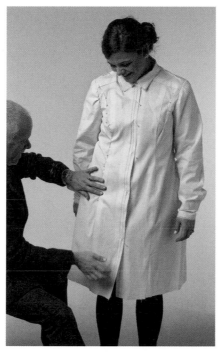

1. To give more shape under the bust, pin out the excess at the princess seam under the bust.

2. Continue pinning down the garment, tapering the seam from under the bust until there is no alteration at the hem. This makes the skirt hang smoothly.

TIP // IN CONVENTIONAL FITTING, THE FLARE ON A FLARED SKIRT BEGINS AT THE FULLEST PART OF THE HIPS, WHICH I BELIEVE IS TOO LOW. I LIKE THE FLARE TO START 2 IN. TO 3 IN. HIGHER BECAUSE THE SKIRT WILL BIND OR PULL HORIZONTALLY AT THE START OF THE FLARE IF IT'S AT THE FULLEST PART OF THE HIPS. BEGINNING THE FLARE ABOVE THE HIPS ALLOWS THE SKIRT TO FALL SMOOTHLY, WHICH IS MORE FLATTERING.

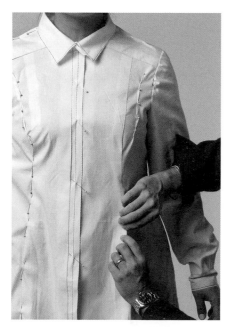  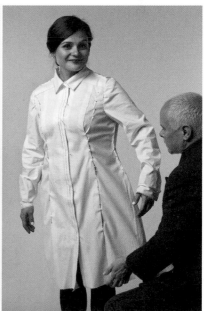

3. Pin the other front vertical seam the same way to create a balanced appearance. Smooth out the skirt to help it hang freely.

4. After correcting the front seams on both sides, it's clear that there is still too much fabric at the waist. I pin some shape into the side seams for Evamarie. This alteration fades to nothing at the hipline, because the skirt is slightly flared.

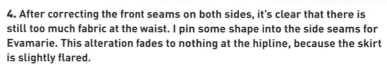

PIN OUT THE WRINKLES

SLEEVE LENGTH

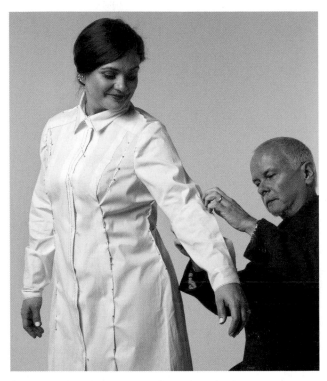

1. Now I will address excess sleeve length, sleeve circumference, and comfort.

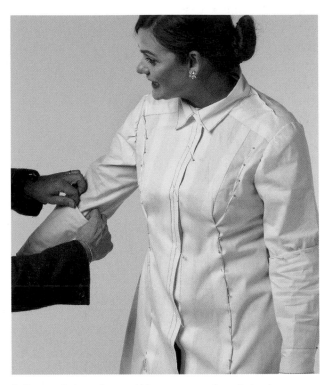

2. Evamarie has plenty of bicep room and can bring her arm up to 45 degrees, so the fit of the sleeve is good.

3. The cuff should sit in front of the prominent bone on the wrist when the arm is bent.

THE PINNED-OUT MUSLIN

Here's Evamarie in her first muslin with all the pinned alterations. Now, off comes the muslin and to the sewing room it goes. The alteration process involves marking the pins, taking the muslin apart—as needed—and transferring the changes to the paper pattern to preserve them for future use.

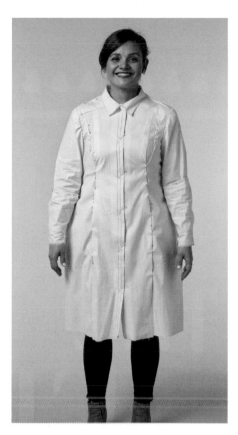

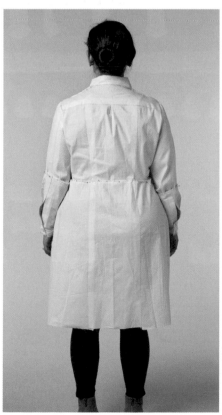

ALTER
THE
PATTERN

> "Compare the **altered muslin** to the original—it's **hard to believe** how **different** the same garment can look."

IN THIS SECTION, ALL THE PIECES COME TOGETHER, AND YOU learn how to transfer the pinned muslin adjustments to a paper pattern. The order of adjusting the pattern and correcting the muslin may be different from the order in which you pinned.

In Part II you learned how to read the wrinkles and pin them. In Part III, I'll walk you through the steps of correcting the changes. You will probably want to read through Part III to grasp the pulse of the process. As you go along, you will see how, in many ways, the process is repeated regardless of the alteration: First, you mark the pins' placement on the muslin, called setting the alterations. Next, clean up the marks, make them the right shape, and be sure they are clear and easy to see. Then correct that muslin section and transfer the changes to the paper pattern.

At the end of the process, you will have a muslin that fits and a matching corrected pattern. If the muslin needs some fine-tuning at that point, repeat the process again: Pin out the wrinkles, mark the pins, transfer the changes to your pattern, alter the muslin, and check your fit.

Mark both sides of the pinned muslin seam along the pins. I use two ways—hash marks and pin marks. Hash marks are used when the information you want to save is included in a fold. The example used here is on a sleeve, where the amount to be removed is folded inside the sleeve. By hash marking over the folded edge, you capture the folded edge perfectly. When you remove the pins, you can draw a well-defined line along the good edge of the hash marks to use to reference your perfect fit.

Sometimes hash marks don't work for the type of pinning that took place. For example, if a dart is pinched up, leaving a fin on the outside of the garment, you'll mark along the pins on both sides of the fin, pleat, or seam. When you remove the pins, you will have a dashed line marking the shape of the alteration, which you can then re-mark with a ruler.

When you have the altered muslin, compare it to the way the muslin looked before the changes. It's hard to believe how different the same garment can look. The results are so good you'll never again think that making a muslin is extra work. It's extra reward!

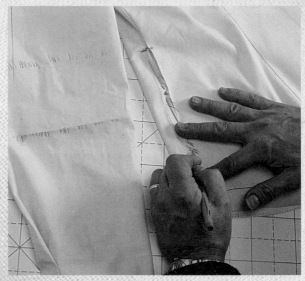

Hash marks are roughly parallel lines made perpendicular to the fold.

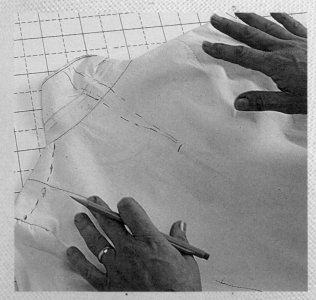

Marking along the pins gives you a dashed line showing the alteration.

CAROL

After pinning Carol's muslin, I "set" the alterations by marking the pin locations on the muslin. I either mark along the pins with a soft no. 2 pencil or draw hash marks over the seam. You'll see both ways demonstrated here. Use the method that works best for you.

SET THE CORRECTIONS ON THE MUSLIN

SLEEVE LENGTH

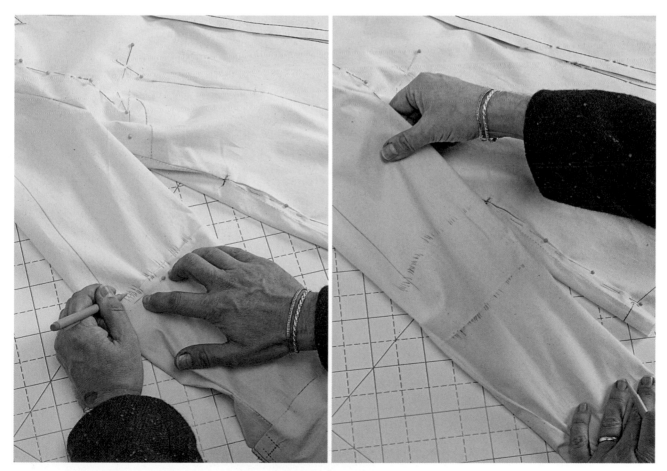

1. To set the corrections, I make hash marks across the folded edges of the alterations, beginning with the easiest one—the sleeve length. Unpin and open the sleeve. You can see the amount of length I will remove between the rows of hash marks.

SET THE CORRECTIONS ON THE MUSLIN

SIDE SEAM

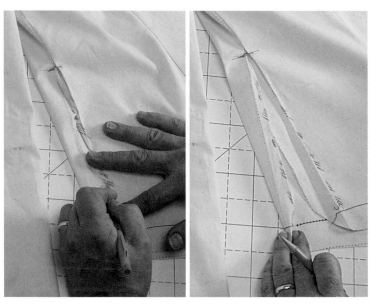

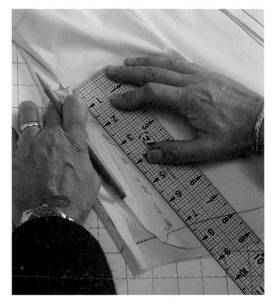

1. Next comes the side seam. Make hash marks across the alteration here as well. Unpin the alteration to reveal the side seam adjustment needed.

2. Use a ruler to mark an accurate line along the hash marks on the muslin. This makes transferring the markings to the paper easier.

BUST PLACEMENT

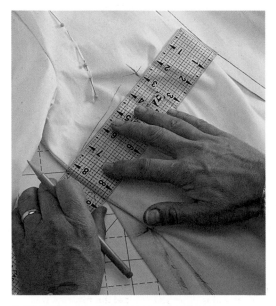

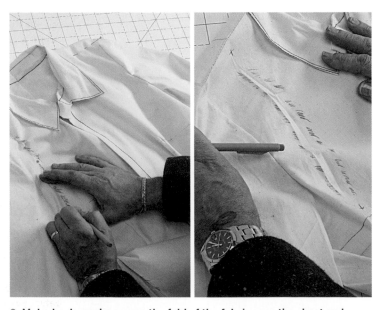

1. Mark the new dart placement and apex.

2. Make hash marks across the fold of the fabric over the chest and remove the pins. Spread the muslin to reveal the alteration needed.

What Is the Bust Point?

When I refer to the bust point, I mean the apex of the bust. It is the fullest circumference horizontally and marks a division vertically. The bust point determines dart placement, but the bust point is not the dart point. The dart length is 1 in. to 1½ in. shorter than the actual bust point. (For more information about fitting a bust, see p. 227.)

To position a body's bust point on a pattern, measure from the shoulder seam at the side of the neck to the bust point. Mark this distance on the pattern. Measure between the bust points, and draw a horizontal line half this length perpendicular to the center-front line from the first mark. That is your bust point.

SHOULDER SLOPE

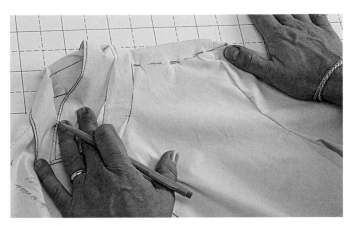

1. On the front, mark the pins on both sides of the garment along the left shoulder to mark the new left shoulder seam.

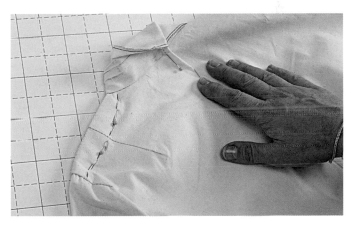

2. Turn the muslin over and mark along the pins on the back left shoulder seam. This alteration impacts the left side collar length as well.

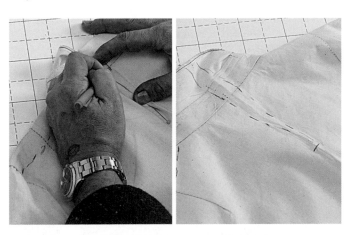

3. Mark the alteration at the center back on the body and collar before you remove the pins. Spread to reveal the alteration at the center back.

DISASSEMBLE THE MUSLIN IF NEEDED

The easiest way to transfer the alterations from the muslin is to take the muslin apart. The marking process involves opening seams and removing parts, so depending on the number of alterations, your muslin may already be almost apart. I mentioned previously to sew a muslin with the longest stitch, and this is why—it makes the job easier now.

A Pattern for an Asymmetrical Body

For an asymmetrical figure, a pattern must have a different right and left side.

But in the industry, commercial patterns are drafted for the right side of a dress form—the center front is to the right of the side seam; the center back is to the left. This is how I will proceed: *with the right side of the pattern having the center front to the right of the side seam.*

The pattern's left side temporarily mirrors the right side. I draft a corrected left front and back and join them to the right sides along the appropriate center seams to make a complete pattern.

CORRECT THE PAPER PATTERN

SLEEVE

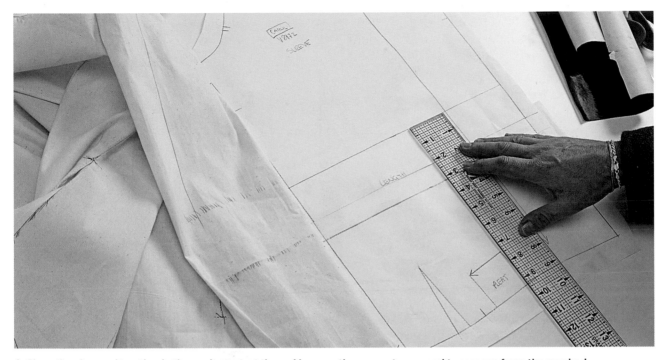

1. Since the sleeve alteration is the easiest, start there. Measure the amount you need to remove from the marked muslin, and mark a parallel line that distance above the horizontal adjustment line on the pattern.

2. Fold the paper, matching the two parallel lines, then tape the paper together. True the seamlines. Truing is regarded as a no net change because we are correcting for distortion.

3. Remove the sleeve if you haven't already and open the side seams. Remove the collar and open the shoulder seams.

4. Open the darts.

5. With the muslin in pieces, I can transfer the markings to the paper pattern and adjust the pattern.

CORRECT THE PAPER PATTERN BACK

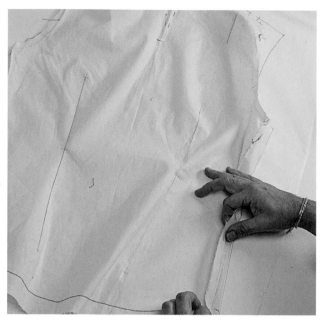

1. I begin with the muslin back because it is all in one piece. Align the muslin stitching lines with the pattern and pin them together. Remember, the pattern doesn't have seam allowances, but the muslin does. The pattern also has wide paper edges around its seamlines.

2. Slip tracing carbon underneath the muslin, face down over the pattern positioned face up.

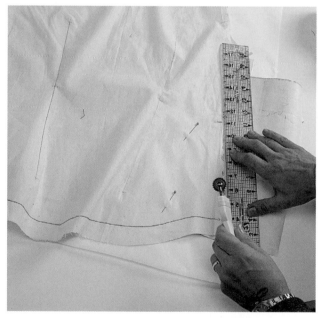

3. Transfer the new seamline onto the paper with the tracing wheel. If you want straight lines, use a ruler. If the new seamline is outside your original paper pattern, you will be glad for the extra paper around your pattern!

4. When you fold the muslin back, you can see the alteration clearly on the pattern.

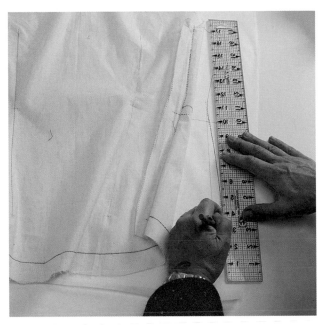

5. Draw neatly over the finished stitching line to make it easier to see.

Patternmaker's Language

Follow this technique professional patternmakers use: When you can't erase a line, make double dashes through it along the length. This is code to say the line is canceled. To avoid confusion, make double "0's" (zeros) to indicate the new line.

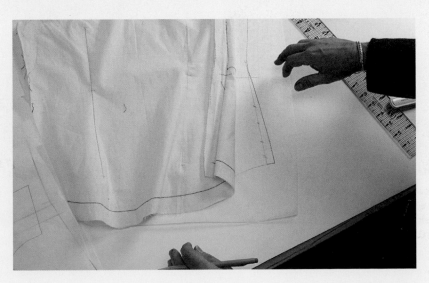

CORRECT THE PAPER PATTERN BACK

NARROW THE BACK THROUGH THE SHOULDERS

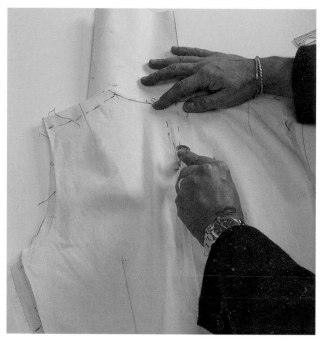

1. Pin the muslin to the pattern at the shoulders, matching the stitching lines. Slip tracing carbon underneath the muslin and transfer the alteration to the paper.

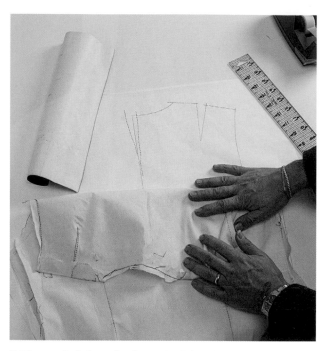

2. The needed alteration is marked, forming what looks like a dart. I will fix this because I do not want a dart down the center of the back.

3. Since this alteration is a long wedge shape that tapers to nothing at the hem, the easiest way to make the alteration is to untape or cut the paper along the center-back line, overlap it at the top center back to remove the wedge, and taper the alteration to zero at the hem.

4. Since the center-back alteration is complete, I fold the paper along the center back and transfer the side seam alteration to the left side of the pattern. (I altered the right side earlier.)

SHOULDER CHANGES

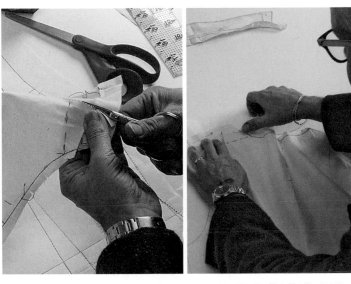

1. Open the shoulder dart on the muslin. Align the left shoulder of the muslin on the pattern, and pin.

2. Place the tracing carbon under the muslin and trace the new left shoulder seam.

SHIFT AN ARMHOLE

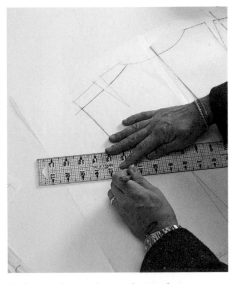

1. Since I lowered the shoulder seam, I also need to lower the entire armhole. Make an armhole template and position it so the armhole matches the new shoulder. The armhole and side seam intersection should align perfectly. Secure the template to the pattern.

2. Use tracing carbon and a tracing wheel to trace the template armhole on the pattern. Remove the template. The alteration is transfered to the pattern. Now go over the carbon lines in pencil to complete the alteration.

NOTE: Notice that I haven't changed the back dart length on the left side, and I kept the vanishing point at the same place as on the right side. Having both darts end at the same spot on each respective side creates the illusion of symmetry.

CORRECT THE PAPER PATTERN BACK

ALTER THE BANDED COLLAR

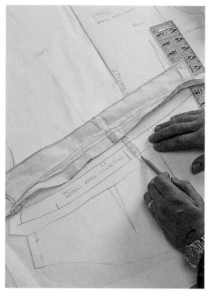  

1. Since the collar band joins to the back, I want to correct it next. Mark the amount removed from the center-back neck during the fitting with two parallel lines on the collar band.

2. Repeat this alteration on the collar flap, aligning it with the lines marked on the band. Be sure the lines are parallel. This is a net loss. Fold the paper along the new lines on both the collar band and the collar flap and tape.

3. Walk the collar band along the neck seamline on the left. Mark the point where the left shoulder seam intersects the neck seam on the band.

 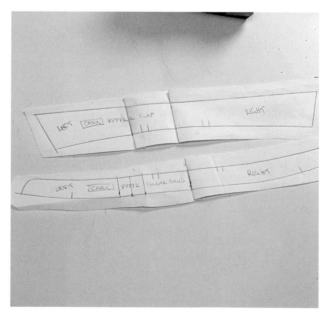

4. Save making the front collar corrections until after fitting the pattern front (p. 145). On the left front, walk the collar band along the neck seam from the center front and mark where the neck seam intersects the left shoulder seam. This makes two points on the collar band. Draft parallel lines as before.

5. Extend these lines up the collar flap. Fold the lines together and tape closed. This produces a collar that is asymmetrical and that will fit Carol's figure.

CORRECT THE PAPER PATTERN FRONT

Once the back corrections are finished, move to the front. I begin with the right side. The corrections at the upper chest on the right side will be transferred to the left side before altering the left shoulder.

1. Open the waist dart so the muslin lies flat. Align and pin the muslin's center front and shoulder with the pattern.

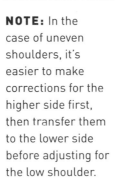

NOTE: In the case of uneven shoulders, it's easier to make corrections for the higher side first, then transfer them to the lower side before adjusting for the low shoulder.

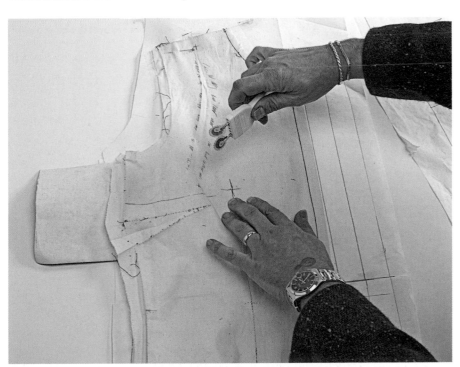

2. Slip tracing carbon under the muslin and trace the hash mark shapes on the chest.

CORRECT THE PAPER PATTERN FRONT

TRANSFER THE BUST MARKINGS

1. Trace the corrected apex and side dart placement. Measure the distance between the original apex and the corrected apex. This is the amount you raise the apex and side dart.

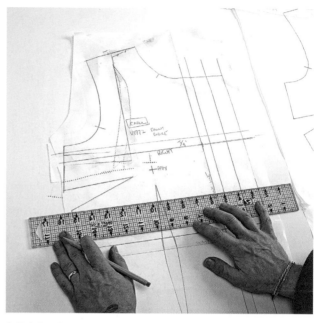

2. Raising the apex and side dart is a no net change—it involves removing paper above the apex and adding the same amount below. This ensures that the dart angle is consistent as well.

Draft a line perpendicular to the center, above the apex level but below the armhole. Draft another line parallel to this one, by the amount you need to raise the apex.

Draft another perpendicular line between the apex and waist level below the dart.

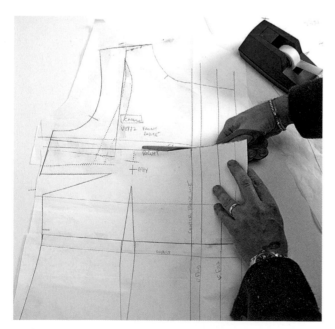

3. Cut the paper along one of the upper lines.

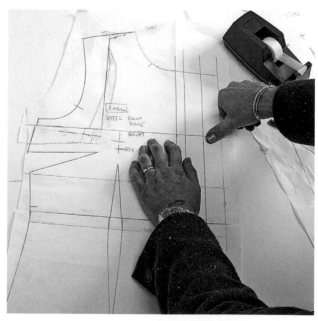

4. Overlap and align it with the second line and tape the two pieces together.

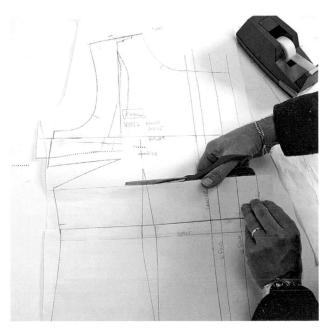

5. Cut the paper on the lower line.

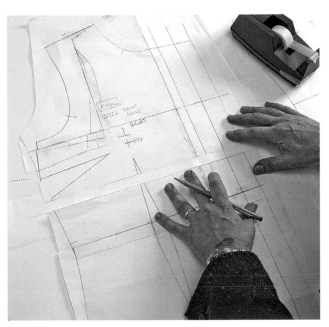

6. Add paper. Draft another line parallel to the cut edge by the amount of the alteration. Align the lower portion of the pattern to the new line and tape the pieces together.

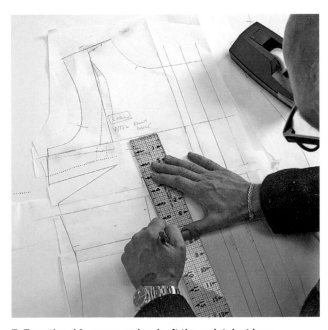

7. True the side seam and redraft the waist dart legs.

CORRECT THE PAPER PATTERN FRONT

REDUCE CHEST FULLNESS

For the correction on the chest area, I use the grid method (see pp. 44–47). This shape is an uneven, double-ended dart that was revealed by the hash marks. Determine the endpoints of the dart and draw a line through them. (Remember from the tutorial that this line does not have to divide the dart equally. It is an axis only.)

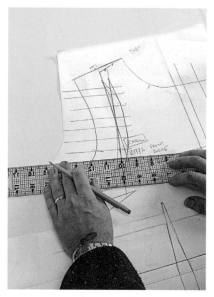

1. Draft perpendicular lines through the dart and toward the nearest seam (in this case, the armhole). The distance between the lines isn't crucial, but ¼ in. to ⅜ in. is good.

2. To remove fabric, measure the width of the line that crosses the dart between the dart legs. Measure that same amount, along the same line, back from the armhole seam, and make a dot on the line.

3. Connect these dots to create the new armhole seam.

4. The new armhole seam needs to be the same length as the original. Measure the original armhole from the underarm to the shoulder. Then measure the adjusted armhole seam from the underarm to the shoulder to see how much longer it is.

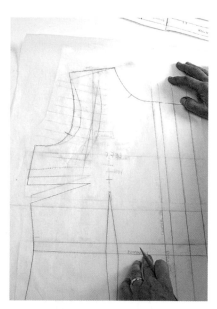

5. Remove the difference between the adjusted armhole and the original armhole from the shoulder and re-draft the shoulder slope. With the alterations to the pattern completed, you can see how Carol's shoulder rotates forward.

TRANSFER CORRECTIONS TO THE LEFT SIDE

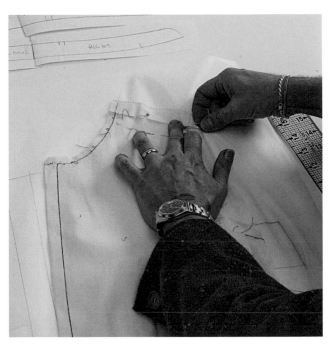

1. After finishing corrections on the right side, transfer these corrections to the left side. Using this thin paper makes transferring corrections easier.

2. Align the center front and shoulder of the left front muslin to the left pattern piece. Pin it to the pattern and slip tracing carbon underneath.

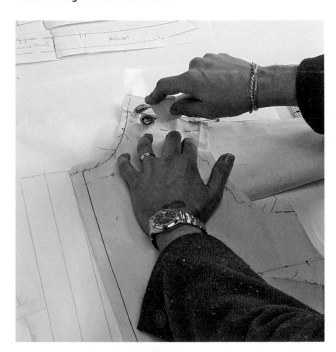

3. Trace the left front shoulder seam.

4. Trace a front armhole template, and adjust the front armhole the same way you adjusted the back armhole.

Making alterations on the left side based on the right side might not fix all the fitting problems in Carol's garment, but it will be a good start. Make the collar adjustment on p. 140. After remaking the muslin based on the first fitting alteration, Carol is ready for her second fitting.

SECOND FITTING: MAKE REFINEMENTS

Carol's muslin has greatly improved after the first fitting, but there are still a few refinements that need to be made.

When viewing the front, you can see that Carol's shirt hangs squarely from her shoulders. Also, her right side fit looks good. There is a small horizontal wrinkle under the arm, but that's the wearing ease I left to allow for lift on the sleeve.

The left side shows a vertical wrinkle, as I expected it would, and horizontal wrinkles under the arm add lift to the sleeve. If you remember, we used the right side for alterations and then created a mirror image for the left side. We then lowered the left shoulder but left the armhole alterations to simplify corrections in the second fitting.

In the back view, you can see that the shirt hangs square. There's a little bit of ripple at the small of the back, which indicates that there needs to be a little more room across the hip area for it to fall smoothly.

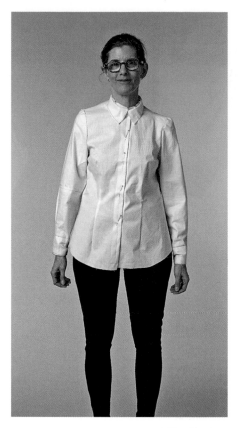

SHOULDER

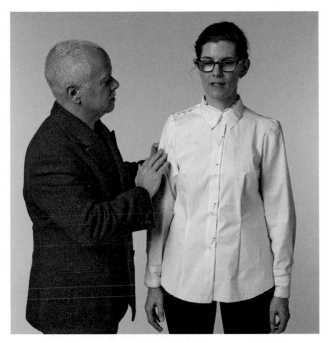

1. The shoulder seams don't reflect the curve of Carol's actual shoulder, and I think a correction is worthwhile since Carol is wearing this shirt without shoulder pads and likely alone or under clothing. If this were a structured jacket with a shoulder pad, the shoulder seam would be left straight.

Recycle Your Muslin

I make hash marks on muslins with a FriXion® erasable ink ballpoint pen. This pen draws a fine line that disappears with a slide of a hot iron. I set the alteration on the muslin, transfer it to the pattern, and then transfer the pattern correction back to the muslin. After I "erase" the marks, the muslin can be reused.

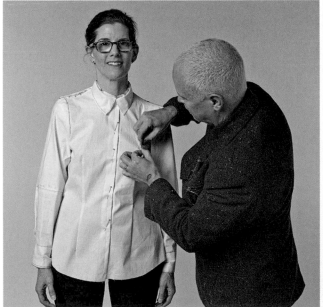

2. On the left side, I pin out the vertical wrinkle, so the muslin sits smoothly in this area. This is a net loss, as I need to remove fabric from this area. I also pin Carol's left shoulder seam to reflect the curve. With those changes, refitting is complete.

FINAL FITTING

Viewing Carol from the right, we see that her shirt sits beautifully on her figure, and the ripples that exist are the normal folds of the fabric as it falls along the figure. From the front and back, you can see that the shirt sits squarely on Carol's shoulders and allows for the normal amount of wearing ease. The pattern is ready to be made from fabric.

NORMA

Norma's first fitting produced this pinned muslin. This muslin now becomes a tool to correct the original pattern.

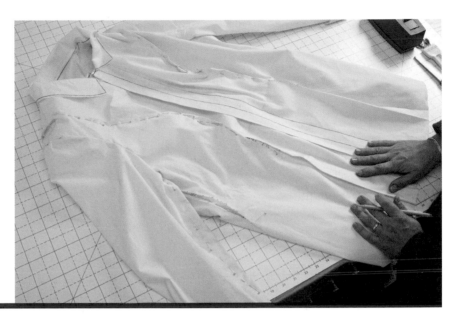

SET THE CORRECTIONS ON THE MUSLIN

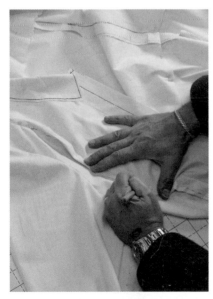

1. Mark the princess seam pins in front, from the shoulder to the waist seam.

2. Next, mark the alteration on the sleeve front, marking at the pins. This alteration decreases the circumference of the sleeve but tapers back to the original armhole.

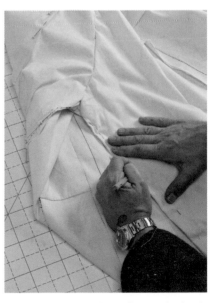

3. Then mark the alteration on the back of the sleeve.

SET THE CORRECTIONS ON THE MUSLIN

SIDE SEAM

1. Continue down from the armhole, and mark the alteration to add space at the waistline on the side seam.

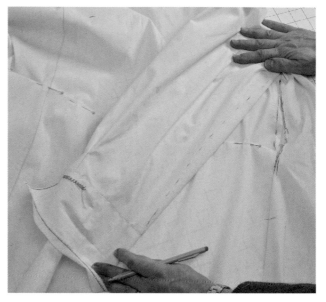

2. Remove the pins to reveal the corrections.

PRINCESS SEAM

1. Mark the alteration at the pins down the back princess seam. Work all the way down to the waist.

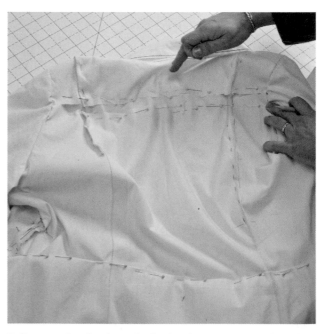

2. Remove the pins from the back princess seam to show the correction.

BACK WAIST

1. Make hash marks across the fold at the back waist.

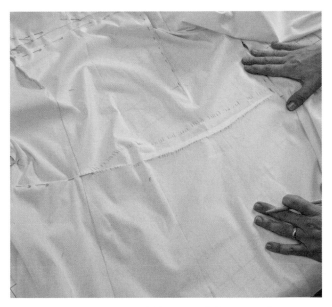

2. Remove the pins and unfold to reveal the correction.

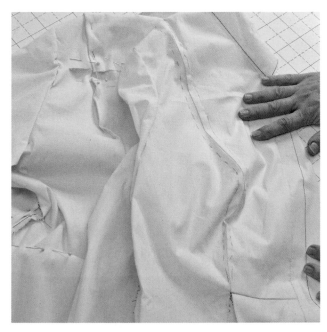

3. Repeat, marking the front princess seam and then removing the pins to reveal the front correction.

DISASSEMBLE THE MUSLIN IF NEEDED

As you go along, some areas can't be sufficiently marked without taking the muslin apart.

BACK PRINCESS SEAMS

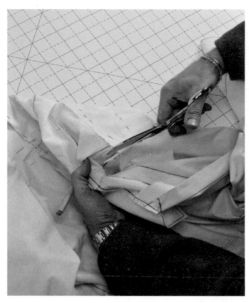

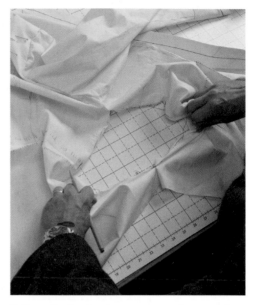

1. On the upper back, cut the horizontal muslin strip vertically along the princess seams. (This strip was inserted across the upper back during the fitting to lengthen the back.) Cutting it enables you to separate the center back and side panels. Don't remove the strip.

2. Open the back princess seams. Remove the sleeve and collar, then remove the side-back panel from the center-back panel.

3. Remark the center-back line on the muslin.

CORRECT THE PAPER PATTERN

UPPER BACK

A condition exists in this adjustment where two alterations cross. I have a net loss on the princess seams, and they cross the cut I made across the upper back, which is a net gain.

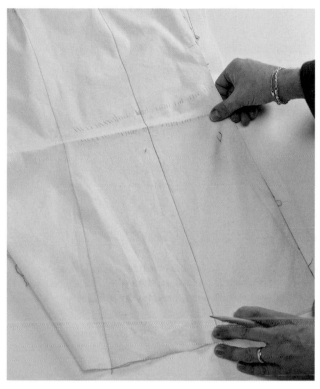

1. Align the center-back panel and hem with the back pattern, and pin.

2. Position a piece of tracing carbon between the muslin and pattern and trace the lower back alteration onto the pattern.

3. Pin the upper center-back panel section to the pattern. This is a half pattern, so align to the center-back line.

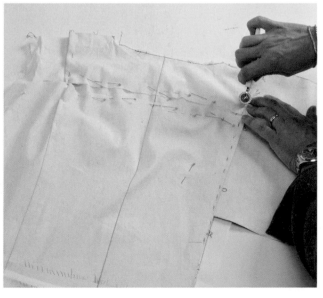

4. Trace the princess seam correction onto the pattern.

CORRECT THE PAPER PATTERN

UPPER BACK (CONTINUED)

5. Mark the top cut edge of the horizontal alteration on the center-back seam and the princess seam on the pattern.

6. Connect the two upper marks at the princess seam and center back with a straight line. This is where you slashed during the fitting and spread the pattern to transfer the alteration.

When this line is marked, measure the distance the muslin spreads at the center back and the princess seams. Note these measurements on the pattern. Then cut the paper along the horizontal line.

7. Position the paper, spread the pattern the correct amount to make the alteration, and tape closed. Redraft the center-back line up to the neck. The horizontal spread caused the original center-back line to angle to the right. I need to correct for distortion here.

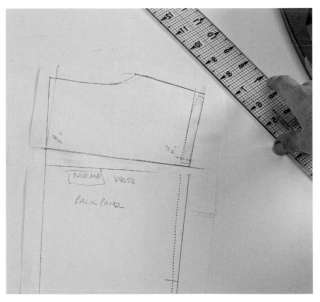

8. Measure how much the original center-back line differs from the new center-back line. Narrow the neck width by that amount and bring the shoulder line back as well. This will keep a straight center-back line that can be cut on the fold.

WAIST

1. Working down to the waist, draw the lines that indicate the correction, fold them out, and tape closed.

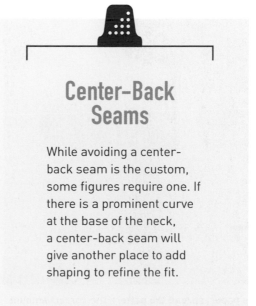

Center-Back Seams

While avoiding a center-back seam is the custom, some figures require one. If there is a prominent curve at the base of the neck, a center-back seam will give another place to add shaping to refine the fit.

CORRECT THE PAPER PATTERN

SIDE-BACK PANEL

1. Pin the side-back panel to the pattern, aligning all the seamlines.

2. Mark the waist correction with tracing carbon and a tracing wheel.

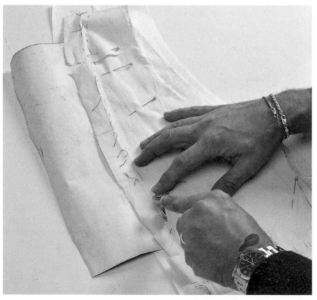

3. Mark the princess seam correction on the pattern. Also, mark the horizontal spread with a cross mark on the princess seam. Go over the corrections in pencil.

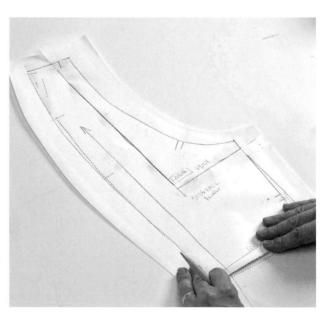

4. Fold out the wedge-shaped alteration at the waist and tape closed.

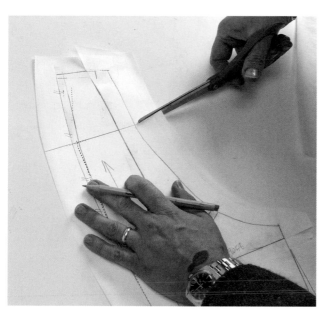

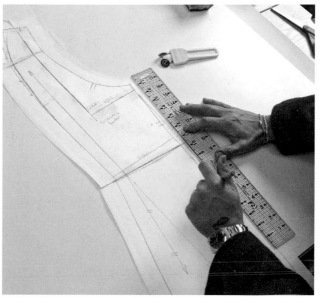

5. Mark a horizontal slash line from the cross mark on the princess seam to the armhole seamline. Cut the paper from the princess seamline to the armhole seamline, leaving a small hinge of the paper attached at both seamlines to form a pivot.

Lay the larger part of the pattern over a separate piece of paper, then spread the alteration amount at the princess line to match the spread along that seam on the center-back panel. Tape the insert to the pattern.

6. To correct for distortion, flatten the point made along the side seam when the waist correction was folded out. I removed about 1/8 in.

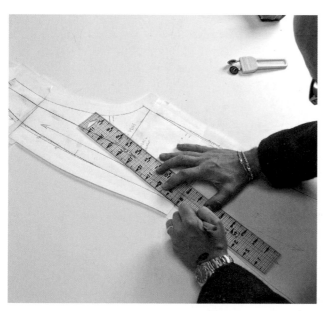

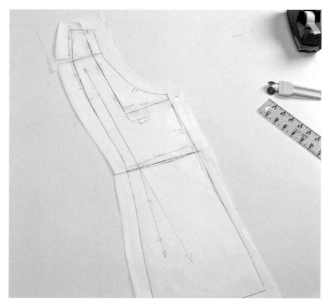

7. Add that 1/8 in. to the princess seam at the waist. This smooths out that curve and creates a no net change for correcting the distortion. Also, smooth out the upper portion of the curve along the princess seam.

8. The completed side-back panel.

CORRECT THE PAPER PATTERN

FRONT

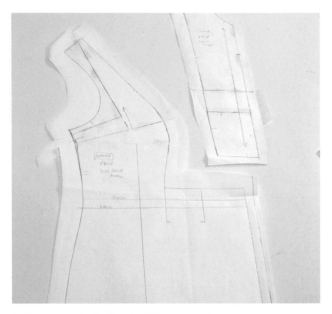

1. Now move to the front of the garment.

2. Align the muslin center front with the pattern center front. Pin the muslin to the pattern. Trace the front princess seam alteration onto the pattern, then go over the alteration with pencil.

SIDE-FRONT PANEL

1. Pin the side-front panel of the muslin to the pattern, matching the stitching lines. Trace the correction onto the pattern, then go over the correction with pencil to complete the alteration.

TIP // I DRAFT A SIDE-FRONT PRINCESS SEAM ⅜ IN. LONGER THAN THE CENTER-FRONT PRINCESS SEAM, THEN EASE THAT AMOUNT IN THE BUST AREA WHEN SEWING THE SIDE TO THE CENTER PANEL. THIS EASING ENABLES THE FABRIC TO SHAPE AROUND THE BUST, CREATING A SOFTER FIT.

TIP // IF YOU NEED TO LENGTHEN OR SHORTEN THE SIDE-FRONT SEAM TO CORRESPOND TO THE CENTER-FRONT SEAM, MAKE THE ALTERATION AT THE SHOULDER END OF THAT SEAM.

SECOND FITTING: MAKE REFINEMENTS

Norma's new muslin fits pretty well. The only correction I need to make is reducing the fabric across the bust at the princess line. I unpinned the seam and took in the excess to make the bust sit smoothly.

I use disappearing ink pens to mark, so I can recycle this muslin after we correct the pattern.

I made second-round alterations in the same way as the first round. In this case, the correction was on the side-front panel. I made hash marks across the front princess seamline and removed the pins to reveal the correction amount to change from the side-front panel. This is a net loss of fabric on that pattern piece.

Lay the side-front muslin panel onto the pattern and trace the alteration onto the paper with the tracing wheel. Redraft the princess seam and check to see if this seamline matches the one on the center-front panel.

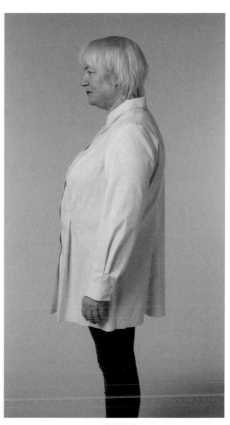

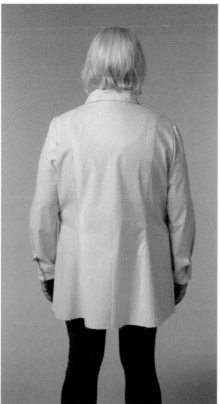

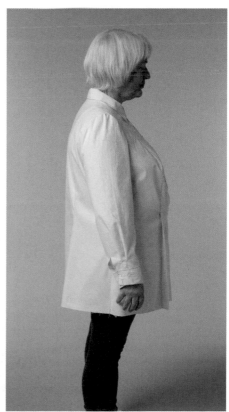

FINAL FITTING

Compare these photos of Norma's finished muslin with those shown on pp. 84–85 to see the progression of this top. You can instantly see how the proper fit is more flattering. The garment itself is more appealing, and, therefore, the wearer is more attractive. Once the fitting and muslin are complete, you have a master pattern that can be used repeatedly in different fabrics for a variety of seasons and looks.

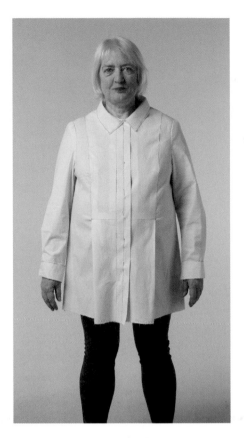
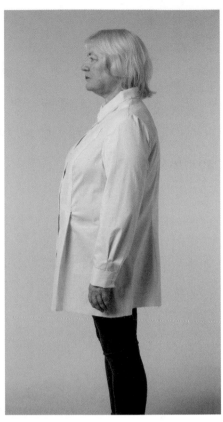
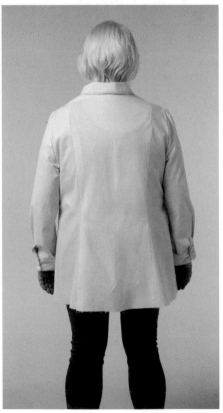
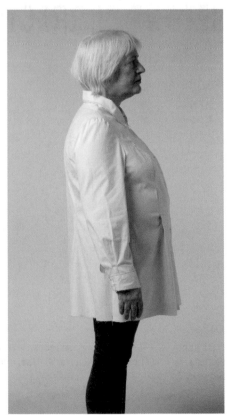

SARAH

Now that I'm finished with Sarah's first fitting, I mark the pinned alterations on the muslin, then transfer those to the pattern.

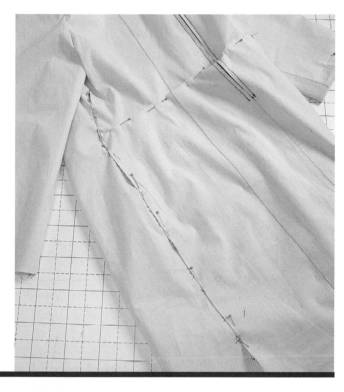

SET THE CORRECTIONS ON THE MUSLIN

1. Beginning at the top, make hash marks along the princess seams from the shoulder to the waist. Also, mark the shoulder seam adjustment. Extend these marks up onto the collar.

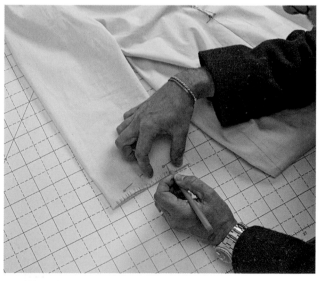

2. Mark the sleeve length.

SET THE CORRECTIONS ON THE MUSLIN

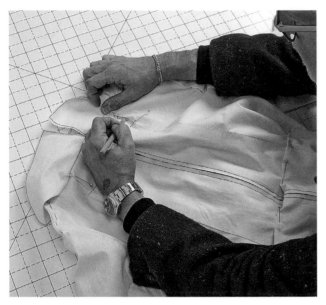

3. At the back neck, make hash marks across the alteration along the princess seam at the neck seam. Make sure to mark the width of this alteration onto the collar.

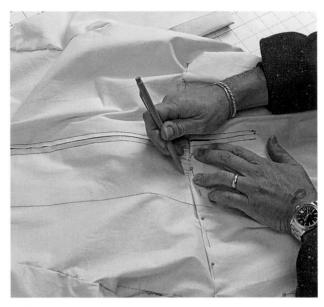

4. Make hash marks across the pins at the waist.

5. Make hash marks down the side seam on the left side to the hem.

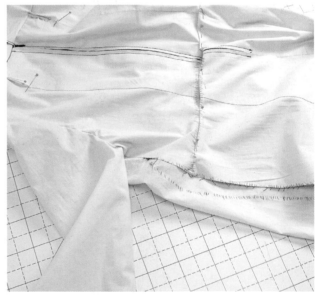

6. Mark and remove the pins down the side seam, at the back neckline, and along the princess seams.

DISASSEMBLE THE MUSLIN IF NEEDED

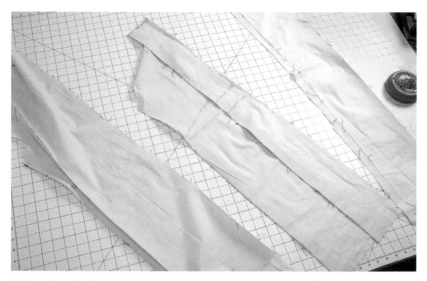

1. To make altering easier, remove first the sleeve, then the collar. Open the remaining seams, separating the muslin pieces.

CORRECT THE PAPER PATTERN

UPPER BACK PANELS

1. At the top of the back panels, remove the excess along the princess line at the neck. This is a simple process of measuring the depth of the adjustment, as well as the length. Once measured, I can transfer the markings to the center-back and side-back panels, and then redraft the seams.

2. Since I'm working with the left side of the muslin, I need to transfer the correction to the wrong side. This is because Sarah's body is asymmetrical and will require different patterns for the right and left sides. With the tracing carbon facing up, use the tracing wheel and trace the corrections.

CORRECT THE PAPER PATTERN

UPPER BACK PANELS (CONTINUED)

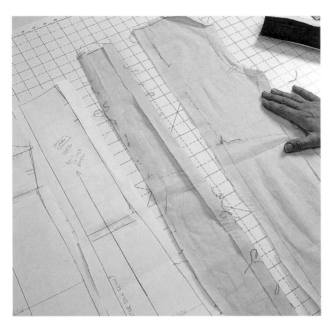

3. Turn the pieces over to reveal the markings.

4. Pin the muslin side panel to the pattern, aligning the stitching lines.

5. Pin the muslin side-back panel shoulder area to the pattern. Trace the new shoulder line onto the pattern.

6. This is what the correction looks like on the pattern.

WAIST BACK PANEL

1. Trace the corrections of the waist onto the side-back panel.

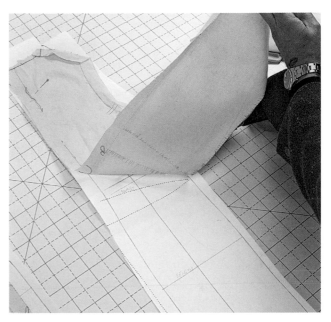

2. Fold the muslin back to reveal the marking.

3. Pin the center-back panel to the pattern.

4. Trace the waist correction onto the pattern.

CORRECT THE PAPER PATTERN

WAIST BACK PANEL (CONTINUED)

5. Here's the correction on the paper.

6. Fold the lines closed—a net loss— and tape to secure. True up the center-back seam and princess seam to correct for distortion.

7. On the side-back panel, fold the wedge-shaped dart closed. Tape to secure.

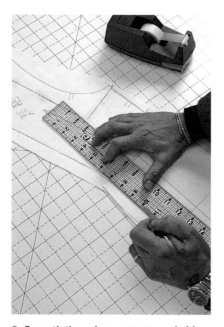

8. Smooth the princess seam and side seam to correct for distortion.

9. With the back pieces corrected, let's move to the front.

FRONT

1. Align the muslin center front with the pattern center-front line and pin the pieces together.

2. Trace the princess seam corrections from the muslin to the pattern, then fold back the muslin to reveal the correction. True the seamline to finish the correction.

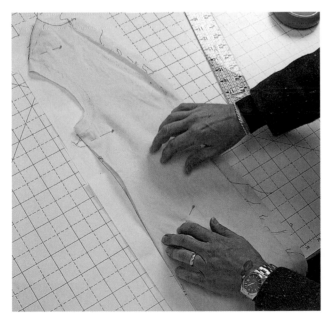

3. Pin the muslin side-front panel to the pattern, aligning the seamlines.

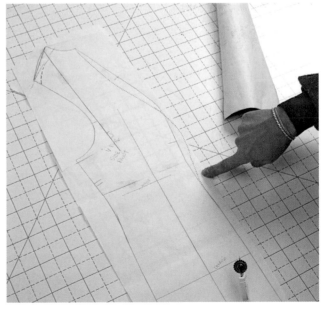

4. Trace the shoulder correction, then trace the princess seamline correction onto the pattern. This is the pattern after the corrections are traced.

CORRECT THE PAPER PATTERN

FRONT (CONTINUED)

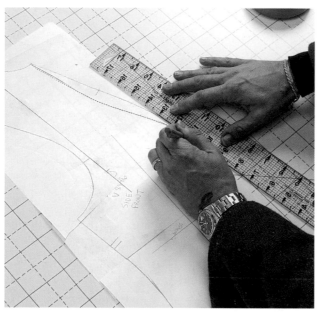

5. Draft the shoulder seam correction and princess seamline correction.

6. Move to the muslin left side to make the correction for the left front hip.

7. Transfer the hip correction to the wrong side of the muslin to reverse the pattern to make an asymmetrical garment with the tracing wheel and carbon.

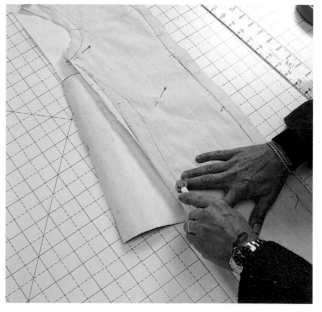

8. Pin the muslin side-front panel to the pattern, then trace the left alteration onto the pattern with the tracing wheel and carbon.

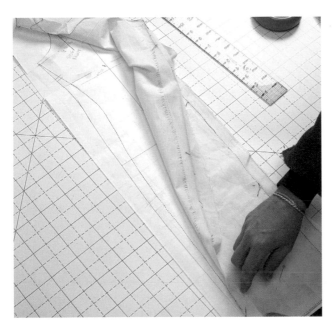

9. This is what the correction looks like.

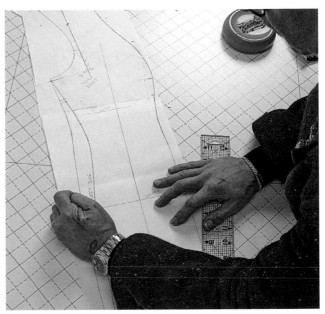

10. Draft the left side seam onto the pattern and label it.

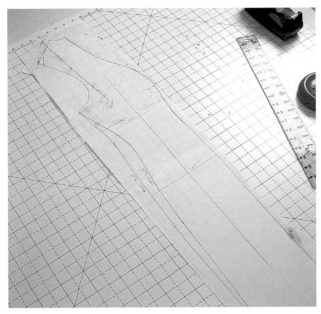

11. Here's the finished correction.

CORRECT THE PAPER PATTERN

COLLAR

1. After the body is completed, the collar is next. Start at the center front and walk the collar neck seam along the bodice neck seam to the princess seamline, then to the new shoulder seam. Mark the point where the new shoulder seam meets the collar.

2. Next, start at the center back and walk the collar along the neckline seam; note the correction amount at the princess seam and where the new shoulder line falls.

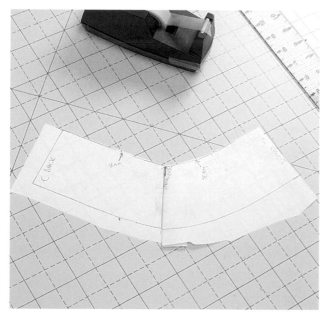

3. Fold out the excess in the collar and tape closed to finish the collar. These adjustments are net losses, folded out of the collar along the parallel lines. True the curves, a net loss.

SHORTEN THE SLEEVE

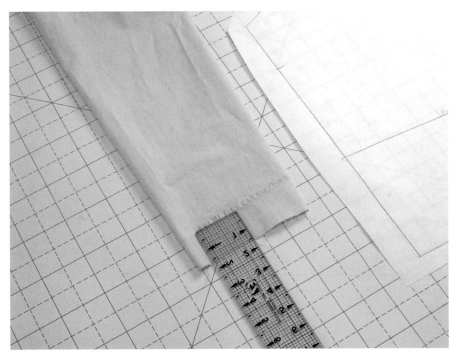

1. This is a straight sleeve, with no elbow dart, so the easiest way to shorten it is just to trim it at the cuff. This is how I correct the length of this sleeve.

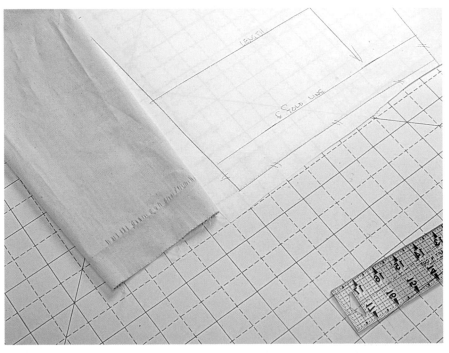

2. Measure the amount you wish to shorten the sleeve and mark it on the pattern. Draft a new cuff line to finish recording the alteration.

SECOND FITTING: MAKE REFINEMENTS

Since Sarah is slightly asymmetrical, the pattern needs separate alterations on the left and right sides. I have cut a whole pattern (full right and left sides) for these corrections, as this is easier and less confusing.

As before, it is easiest to begin from the top down. First, pin-fit, and then mark the corrections on the muslin. Once that's done, you can take the muslin apart.

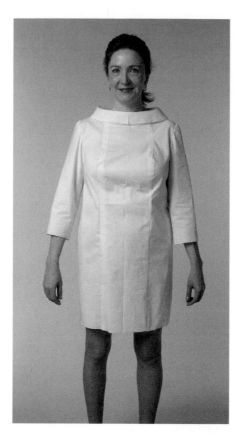

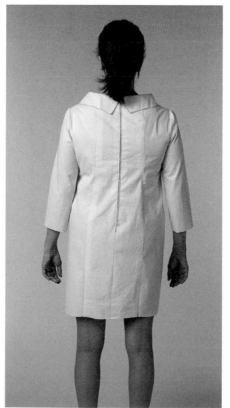

SHOULDERS AND ARMHOLES

1. I repinned the sleeve onto the armholes on both sides. This eliminated the vertical ripples near the armhole and brought the shoulder seam up to Sarah's actual shoulder. The hash marks across the armhole seam show what the new armhole seam will look like. The sleeve remains the same—just the bodice armhole is altered.

This is a simple transfer; match the muslin shoulders and original muslin armholes to the corresponding front and back pattern pieces. Then trace the alterations onto the pattern.

2. Working down the pattern, I adjust the right side first. Wrinkles at the front princess seam indicate the need to take in the side-front panel. Again, pin, mark, remove pins, and trace the alteration from the muslin to the pattern to alter the pattern.

3. I mark the amount that was pinned out at the waist on the right side-back and right center-back patterns to pick up the slight wrinkle below Sarah's right waist. Fold this out and tape it closed by matching the lines. On the center-back panel, this alteration looks like a wedge—fold out the amount, tapering to nothing at the center back.

Once these two alterations to the right side are finished, I need to add the amount we folded out at the waist as additional length at the hem. This, in the end, is a no net change alteration.

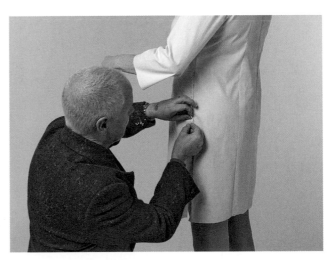

4. Moving to the left side, I repinned the side seam to fall closer to the back. Transfer the alteration to the left side-front and side-back pattern pieces below the waist. Redraft the side seam, which takes from the skirt back and adds to the skirt front.

You're finished with the second fitting alterations.

FINAL FITTING

Here are the final results of fitting the muslin. Compare these images with the first images on pp. 94–95. This is a clear picture of the benefits of fitting. The final garment will be even more attractive, and by going through these steps, the next time you sew this garment, the process will be much faster and easier. Plus, the result will improve both looks and comfort.

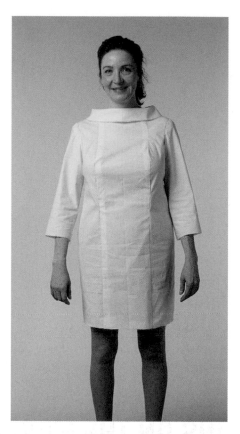

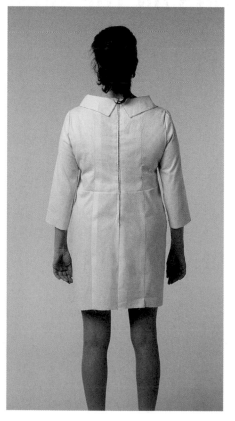

ROSANN

With Rosann's dress all pinned, I move to my worktable to transfer the alterations to the pattern.

SET THE CORRECTIONS ON THE MUSLIN

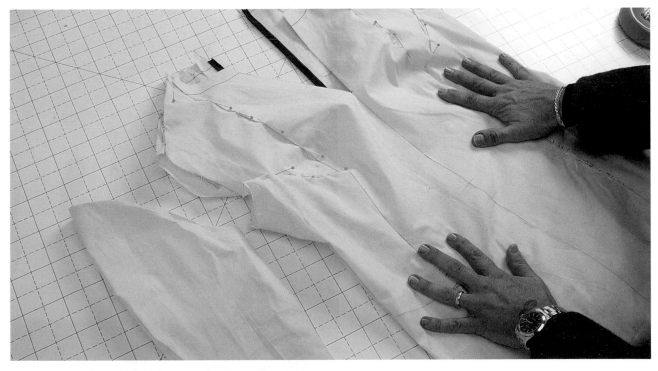

1. As with the other muslins, I remove the sleeve first.

SET THE CORRECTIONS ON THE MUSLIN

BODICE

1. Beginning at the shoulders, mark the pin corrections on the muslin with pencil. This photo shows marking the right shoulder. I mark the front and back shoulder at the same time.

2. Open the shoulder seam, and use a ruler to draft a clean line indicating the change. I mark the front first, then the back.

3. Next, working down the bodice front, make hash marks across the princess seam to indicate the changes there. Unpin the muslin.

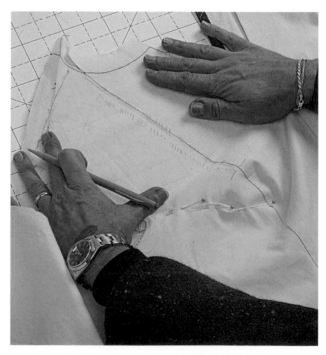

4. This is what the change looks like after unpinning.

5. Next, make hash marks across the dart folded out from the armhole to the princess seam. Unpin the dart and open.

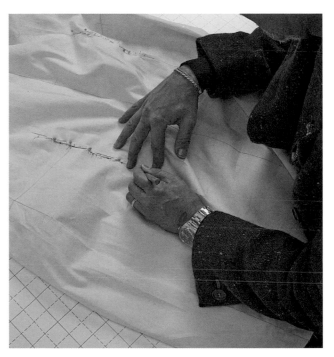

6. Working down the front, make hash marks over the correction along the princess seam in the waist region. Remove the pins.

7. This is what the correction at the waist looks like.

SET THE CORRECTIONS ON THE MUSLIN

BACK

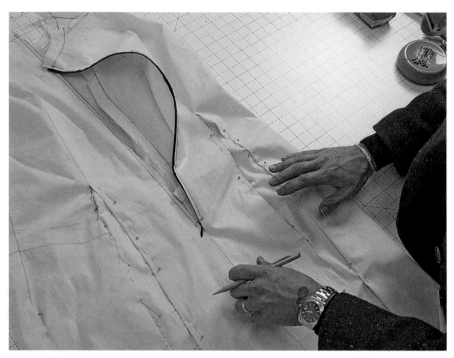

1. Move down the back. This is where I pinned the muslin along the princess seams at the hipline when initially fitting Rosann's muslin. This alteration is a net gain of fabric, and visually you can see exactly where it adds to the muslin.

2. Make hash marks along the side seams as well, to mark the corrections.

DISASSEMBLE THE MUSLIN IF NEEDED

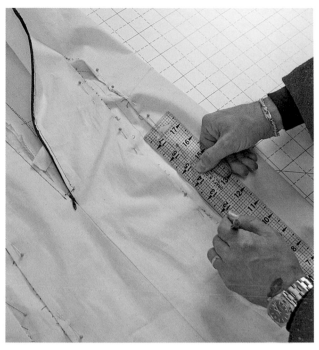

1. I need to create a new princess seam on the muslin patch. I draft the seam midway between the existing seam instead of making the alteration to the side panel. Often, alterations made to a princess seam are directed to the side panel. In this case, because of this alteration's nature, splitting the alteration between the center and side panels produces more flattering results.

2. Once the new princess seamline is drawn, cut along the line to separate the center-back panel from the side-back panel. Don't remove the pins holding the muslin patch to the panel.

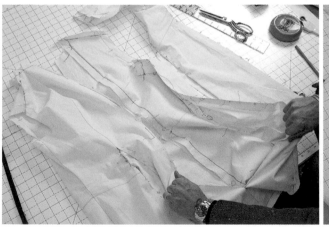

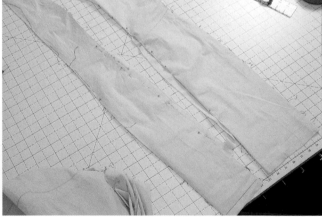

3. Open the rest of the princess seam above the alteration to separate the center panel from the side panel. Having the back pieces apart makes altering easier. Open the princess seams on the front as well.

CORRECT THE PAPER PATTERN

BODICE

1. With the front pieces apart, I am ready to make pattern adjustments. Starting with the side panel, pin the muslin stitching lines to the corresponding stitching lines on the pattern.

2. Slip tracing carbon underneath, then use the tracing wheel to transfer all corrections from the muslin to the pattern.

3. Here you can see the shoulder alteration and new princess seam.

FIT THE FRONT

1. This is the dart that needs to be folded out in the pattern. The dart transfers to the princess line.

2. Pin together the muslin and pattern at the waist area on the upper side panel on the princess seam.

3. Use tracing carbon and a tracing wheel to transfer the alteration.

4. Pin the lower muslin side panel to the corresponding lower pattern piece.

CORRECT THE PAPER PATTERN

FIT THE FRONT (CONTINUED)

5. Use the tracing wheel and carbon to transfer this alteration.

6. Align the pattern's lower side panel with the upper side panel along the horizontal seamline, and pin.

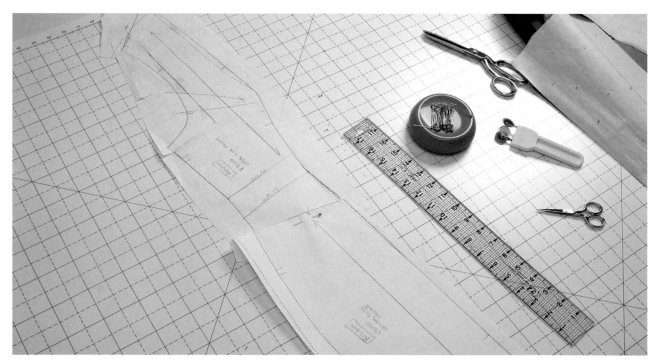

7. Correct for distortion in the pattern by smoothing the princess seamline.

ARMHOLE

1. At the armhole, draft two dart legs along the hash marks. Fold out this dart.

2. Fold the two lines together to create a net loss. Tape the fold closed. True the corrected seamlines for the armhole and princess seams.

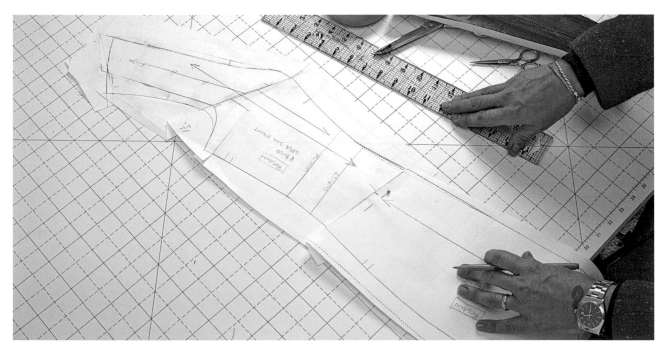

3. Smooth out all other seamlines. Establish a new grainline by extending the original lower side panel grainline up and through the upper side panel. Remove the original grainline from the upper side panel. Then unpin the lower side panel from the upper side panel. This section is complete. There are no corrections to the center-front panel.

CORRECT THE PAPER PATTERN

BACK

1. Lay out the center-back panel and the bodice and skirt side-back pieces. Combine the two side-back panel pieces.

2. Before I can alter these pieces, I need to add paper to the side- and center-back panel princess seamlines below the waist.

3. I chose to use the left side of the muslin because Rosann's left hip is slightly higher than her right hip. Using the higher hip in adjusting the pattern will make the refit less work, as there is more fabric on the higher hip seam. Therefore, I need to transfer the correction to the opposite side of the muslin. Slip carbon face up under the muslin and trace the correction to the wrong side. Now the left side has a pattern on the wrong side of the muslin.

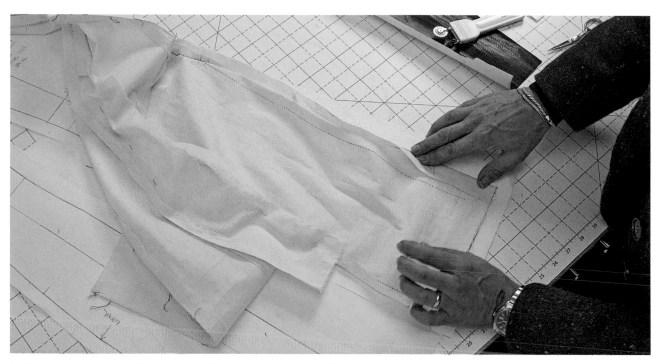

4. Start with the combined side panels. Pin the muslin, wrong side up, to the pattern along the original side seam.

5. Use the tracing carbon and wheel to trace the correction onto the pattern.

6. Here is the correction marked on the pattern. To finish it, trace over the alteration in pencil, then true the side seam.

CORRECT THE PAPER PATTERN

BACK HIP

1. Next, alter both princess seam sides at the hip. Pin the muslin center-back seamline to the pattern. Smooth the muslin across the pattern and pin the opposite side to the pattern. Slip tracing carbon under the patch and trace along the cut edge of the muslin patch. This is the new princess seam.

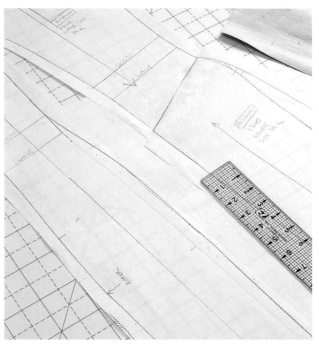

2. Remove the muslin and redraft the new princess seam on the center panel to the corrected markings.

3. Pin the side-back panel to the pattern, aligning the side seam and smoothing out the muslin toward the princess seam.

4. Trace the muslin cut edge on the side-back panel to transfer the alteration to the piece.

5. Split the paper added at the hips to separate the side panel from the center panel. Walk the two princess seamlines together to ensure they are the same length. If they don't match, split the difference at the hem. They should be the same since they started out being the same line.

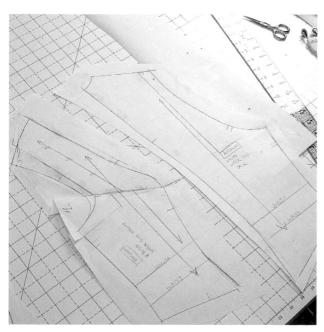

6. Remove the tape to separate the side panel pieces. The back alterations are complete.

SLEEVE

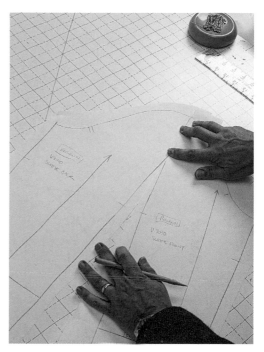

1. Working with the sleeve, first tape the front and back together.

2. Measure the sleeve cap seam length from the front underarm to the center seam. Mark the distance on the sleeve pattern.

CORRECT THE PAPER PATTERN

SLEEVE (CONTINUED)

3. Measure the back sleeve cap seam length from the back underarm to the center seam, and mark the amount on the sleeve pattern.

4. Tape together the upper side-back and upper side-front bodice pattern at the shoulder seam.

5. Measure the length of the back armhole and mark the amount on the sleeve pattern. Measure the length of the front armhole and mark the distance on the sleeve pattern.

6. Now compare the measurements recorded on the sleeve pattern. I'll move the position of the back underarm seam to match the back bodice armhole length. This no net change makes the sleeve underarm seam match the bodice side seam.

7. Tape the underarm seam on the sleeve pattern closed only to the elbow.

8. Redraft the underarm seam to this new point. Cut the pattern along this new line to move the seam.

Cap Ease Amount

A blouse or dress sleeve needs ½ in. to ¾ in. more cap ease than the bodice armhole. (For a tailored jacket, the amount is 1 in. to 1½ in.—my preferred number is 1¼ in.) If you need to add or subtract to get this relationship, I prefer to raise or lower at the bodice underarm to accommodate the difference.

How this works: For example, if you have ½ in. more cap ease than you need, you can lower the bodice underarm ¼ in. and redraft the armhole. You can also raise the sleeve underarm the same amount. Two times ¼ in. equals the ½-in. correction.

CORRECT THE PAPER PATTERN

SLEEVE (CONTINUED)

9. Tape paper to the sleeve pattern underarm seam and redraft the seam. The first fitting is now finished.

Sleeve Cap

Finding the perfect sleeve cap for a well-fitted armhole requires attention to details. It involves getting a sleeve that is comfortable and good-looking around the arm, enables you to reach and move, and eases into the sleeve cap seam smoothly and easily without pleats or puckers. For more on fitting a sleeve, see p. 230.

SECOND FITTING: MAKE REFINEMENTS

You can see that the alterations from the first fitting give Rosann's dress more shape. Now the fitting continues with another round (or more, if needed).

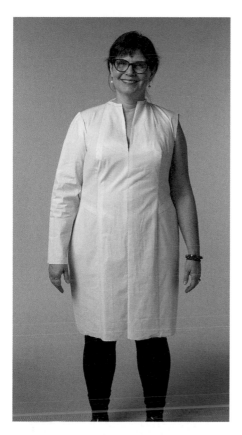

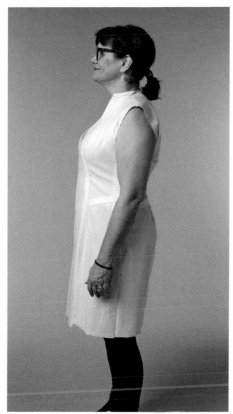

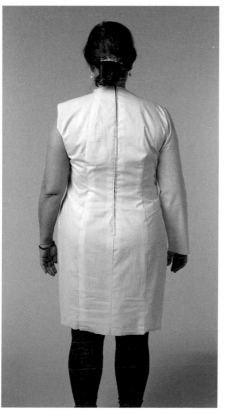

SECOND FITTING: MAKE REFINEMENTS

1. I need to repin Rosann's sleeve to eliminate the diagonal wrinkle at the front shoulder joint. The back waist and side seams need adjustments as well. After making the hash marks on the muslin and taking the muslin apart, the pattern alterations start at the shoulder.

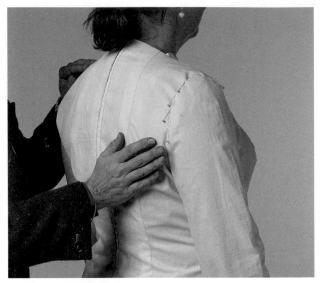

2. The sleeve remains unchanged, but the armhole seam on the front and back bodice gets the alteration. Mark the armhole on the muslin. Lay the corresponding pieces of the muslin onto the pattern and trace out the new armhole. Once the new armhole is drawn, measure it to see how it compares to the armhole measurement on the sleeve.

WAIST

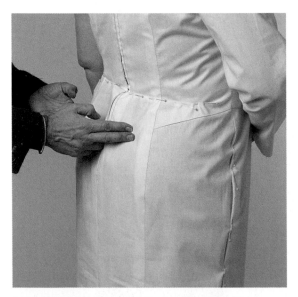

1. Next, move down to the back waist. Fold this alteration in a wedge that crosses the princess seam and tapers to nothing at the side seam. Trace the hash markings onto the pattern pieces, fold the alteration closed, and tape.

SIDE SEAM EXCESS

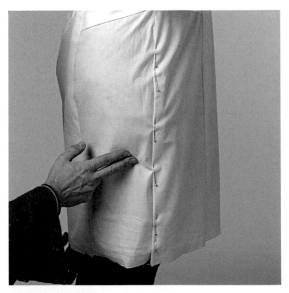

1. Finally, on the back skirt side seam, a new reduction is traced onto the paper, and the seam is redrafted to remove the excess fabric.

We're ready for the final muslin!

FINAL FITTING

Here is Rosann in her finished muslin. Several refinements bring us to this point. Compare these images to the photographs on pp. 104–105. You can see the difference between a commercial pattern almost straight out of the envelope and a well-fitted garment.

It isn't easy to accomplish alterations of this nature by yourself. Having a fitting buddy to help is a perfect plan, but if that's not possible, you can also invest in a custom dress form.

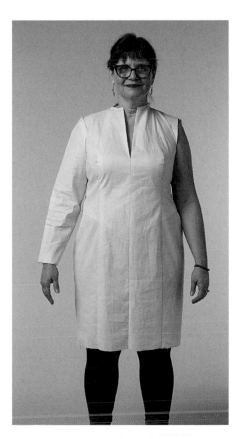
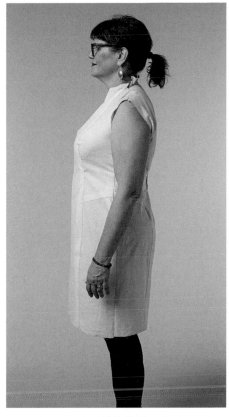
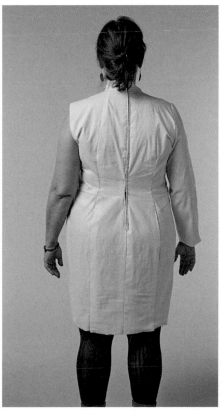
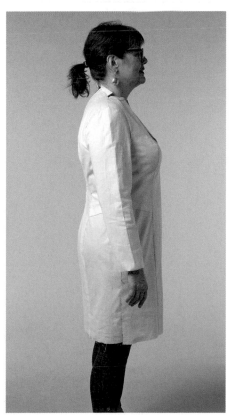

JEANNINE

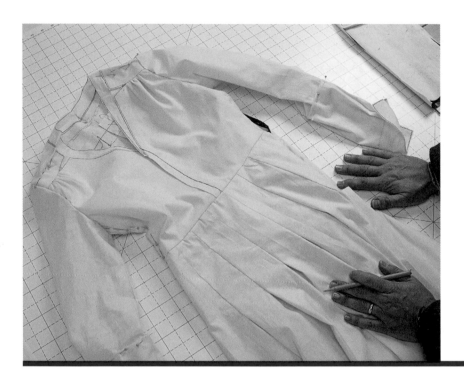

This is Jeannine's pinned muslin after the first fitting. Now those alterations will be recorded in the pattern so I can prepare a second muslin for fine-tuning her fit. I begin alterations with the easiest corrections.

SET THE CORRECTIONS ON THE MUSLIN

SLEEVE LENGTH

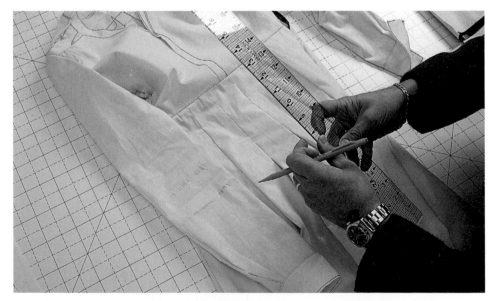

1. Make hash marks across the fold in the muslin sleeve to record the length correction. Remove the pins and unfold the muslin to reveal the revision measurement. Draw along the hash marks to clearly mark the alteration on the muslin.

SIDE SEAM

1. Mark the alteration along the side-front seam pins with a pencil. Turn the muslin over, and mark the alteration along the side-back seam as well. Remove the pins.

NECK

1. Make hash marks over the alteration at the center-back neck. Remove the pins to reveal the correction.

YOKE

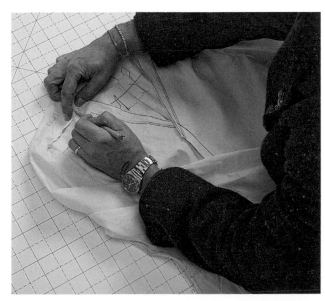

1. At the right shoulder, make hash marks across the fold in the muslin to set the correction. Remove the pins and go over the correction with pencil lines.

2. This is the correction needed on the right shoulder. Repeat the same process for the left shoulder.

SET THE CORRECTIONS ON THE MUSLIN

YOKE (CONTINUED)

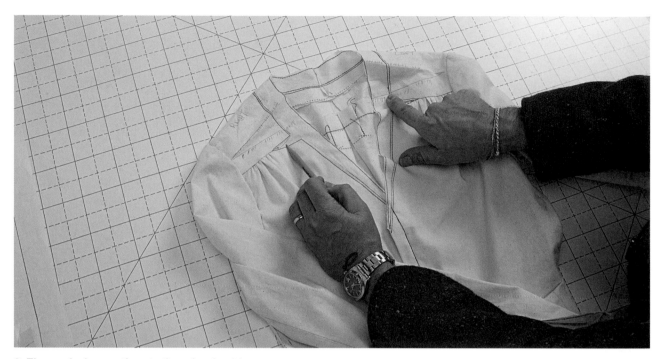

3. The marked corrections to the yoke shoulder.

TIP // WHEN MAKING PATTERN ALTERATIONS THAT OCCUR ACROSS SEAMLINES, IT'S EASIER TO LEAVE THE MUSLIN PIECES SEWN TOGETHER. WHEN ALTERING THE PATTERN, AS YOU WILL SEE, I WILL ATTACH THE PATTERN PIECES ALONG THE SAME SEAMLINES AS THE SEWN-TOGETHER MUSLIN PIECES. THIS MAKES A LESS CONFUSING ALTERATION PROCESS.

4. Remove the sleeves from the bodice, then remove the yoke and neckband from the bodice front and back. Leave the neckband attached at the neckline area of the yoke. This entire section is used to alter the pattern.

CORRECT THE PAPER PATTERN

1. Go over the correction at the center back of the yoke in pencil.

2. Attach the neckband pattern to the neck area of the yoke pattern.

TIP // BECAUSE YOU'RE WORKING WITH A LARGER PIECE OF PAPER, YOU MIGHT NEED TO TRIM IT DOWN BEFORE FOLDING OUT THE SHOULDER ALTERATIONS. THE EXTRA PAPER CAN GET UNWIELDY.

3. I need to make a new yoke pattern piece on fresh paper with the neckband attached. The original pattern has been cut in so many places that rather than tape everything, it's easier to make a new pattern piece before making the alterations. I make a full symmetrical pattern cut on the fold first and then make the asymmetrical adjustments. The easiest way to draft this is to fold the fresh paper in half, place the center back of the yoke on that fold, and, with tracing carbon on both sides of the fresh paper, trace off the entire pattern.

CORRECT THE PAPER PATTERN

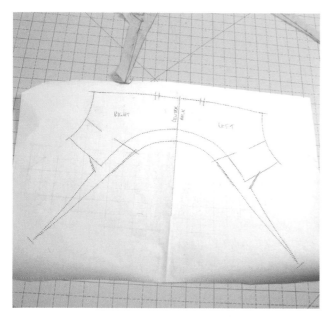

4. Unfold the paper to reveal the entire new pattern piece.

5. Pin the muslin yoke and band section to the new pattern, aligning the seamlines and center back. With tracing carbon and wheel, transfer the alterations from the muslin to the pattern.

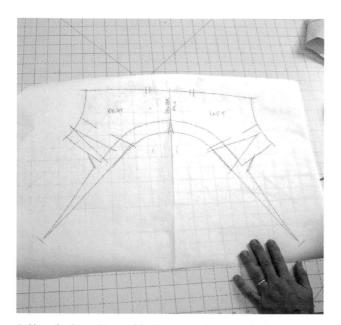

6. Here is the pattern with the corrections marked and ready to alter. See the two wedge shapes.

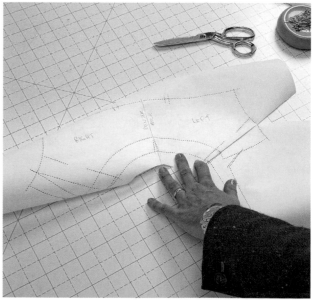

7. Fold out the alterations on one shoulder, then fold out the alterations on the other. Correct for distortion by truing the curves.

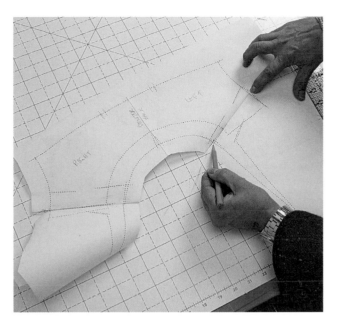

8. The peak created at the armhole is flattened to make a smooth curve. The amount that was flattened was added at the neckline to smooth the neck curve. This is a no net change. I will go over the alteration at the center back in pencil to finish it.

9. Once the corrections are finished, cut apart the shoulder yoke from the neckband to make two separate pieces again.

TIP// I WAS TRAINED TO USE A STRAIGHTEDGE ON CURVES BECAUSE IT IS EXPEDIENT. BUT IF YOU ARE MORE COMFORTABLE USING A CURVE, IT IS EQUALLY ACCURATE.

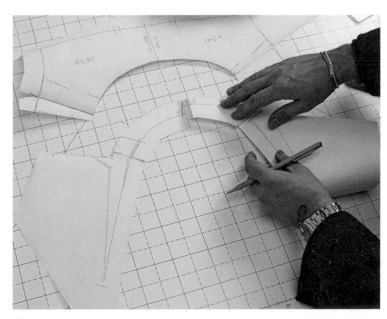

10. Cut the neckband at the center back to make two separate neckband pieces. There will be a seam at the center back. This completes the alteration of the yoke area.

CORRECT THE PAPER PATTERN

BODICE

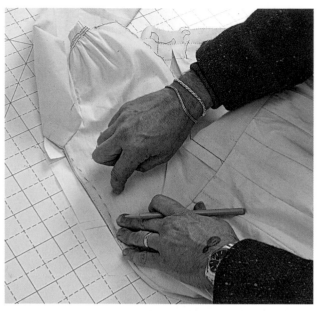

1. Working at the side seam, align the bodice front stitching line with the pattern stitching line.

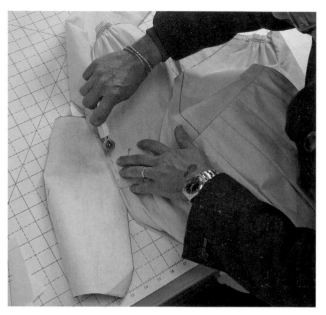

2. With tracing carbon and a wheel, trace the new bodice side seamline onto the pattern.

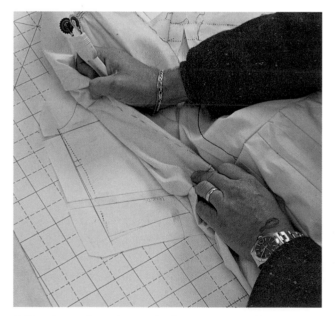

3. Here is the alteration marked on the pattern. Go over the alteration in pencil to finish.

4. Since the back side-seam shape is the same as the front, you can pin the bodice front pattern to the bodice back pattern at the side seams.

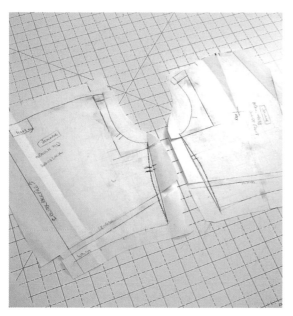

5. With tracing carbon and wheel, trace the front side seam onto the bodice back pattern. Mark the matching notch as well. Go over the alteration in pencil to finish the back to complete the bodice alterations.

TIP // DON'T FORGET TO DRAW HASH MARKS THROUGH OLD SEAMLINES ONCE YOU MAKE ALTERATIONS.

SLEEVE

1. I previously set the sleeve alteration on the muslin. Now it's time to measure the amount to shorten the sleeve and mark it on the pattern length adjustment line. Cut along one of the lines, lay it on top of the other line, and tape closed.

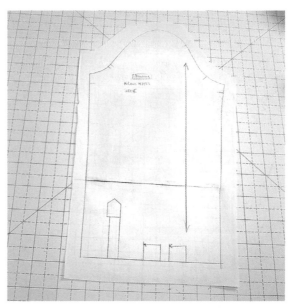

2. True the sleeve side seams, and the altered pattern is finished. Now the muslin is remade, and the fit is fine-tuned in a second fitting.

TIP // WHEN ALTERING THE PATTERN, YOU CAN EITHER FOLD OUT THE NET LOSS OR CUT THE PAPER AND TAPE THE TWO CORRESPONDING LINES TOGETHER. THE EFFECT IS EXACTLY THE SAME.

FINAL FITTING

Sometimes you get it right on the first round of alterations. Jeannine's final muslin fits just as this dress should.

Looking at the front, I can see the bodice hangs squarely and the neckline sits flat. The sleeves are now the proper length.

Looking at the right side, the correction at the shoulder released the diagonal wrinkles at the sleeve cap. This means that the sleeve will be kept constant for the next fitting.

From the back, the dress falls squarely from the shoulders. The shaping at the waist looks good on Jeannine's figure, and there's a reasonable amount of wearing ease across the back.

Looking from the left side, the dress sits well. The issues on the sleeve seam are resolved.

EVAMARIE

Now that I've fitted Evamarie's muslin, it's time to transfer the corrections to the pattern. There are several corrections to make, but the process is always the same.

SET THE CORRECTIONS ON THE MUSLIN

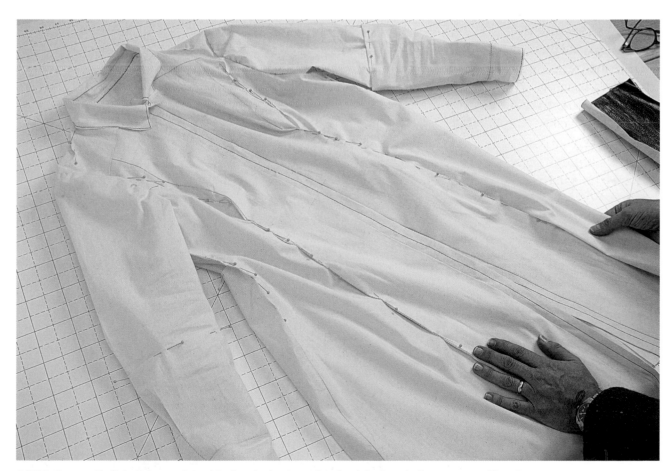

1. With the muslin flat on the cutting table, I make hash marks along the front princess seam. Then I make hash marks across the vertical dart in the upper chest area. Moving down the muslin, I mark the pin placements on the side seam.

SET THE CORRECTIONS ON THE MUSLIN

YOKE SHOULDER

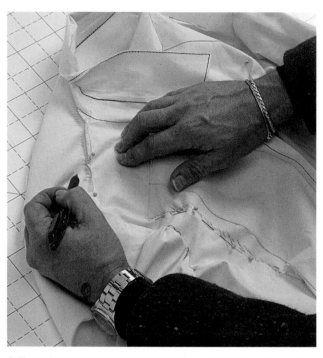

1. Turn the muslin over and mark the correction on the yoke shoulder.

2. Make hash marks across the shoulder correction, as well as across the front bodice corrections.

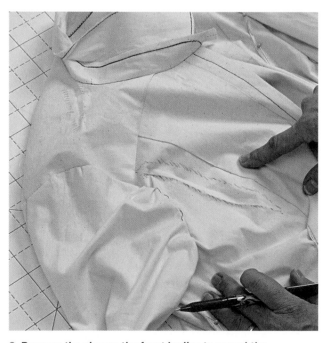

3. Remove the pins on the front bodice to reveal the corrections.

SLEEVE(S)

1. Make hash marks on the sleeve, then remove the pins to reveal the length correction.

WAIST

1. Make hash marks across the back waist alteration.

2. Remove the pins, revealing the correction.

DISASSEMBLE THE MUSLIN IF NEEDED

1. Take out the seams to free up the pieces of the muslin.

CORRECT THE PAPER PATTERN

YOKE

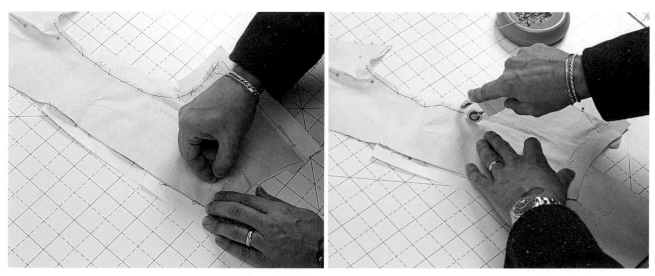

1. Copy the corrections to the pattern. Starting with the yoke, align the stitching lines and pin the muslin to the pattern. Position a piece of tracing carbon under the muslin, face down over the pattern, and use a tracing wheel to transfer the correction to the paper.

CORRECT THE PAPER PATTERN

YOKE (CONTINUED)

2. Cut out the revised pattern and overlap the paper to make the correction.

3. Correct for distortion by truing the armhole seam and neck seam. Since I've altered the yoke shoulders, I have to compensate for that alteration in the collar band.

4. Walk the collar band pattern along the yoke neck seam, starting at the center back and proceeding to the yoke seam above the bust. Mark the shoulder placement.

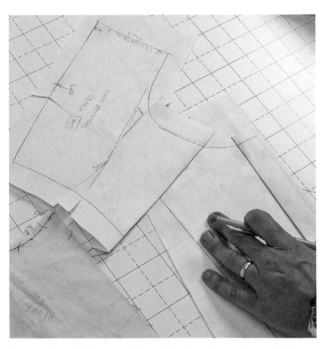

5. Tape the side-front and front band pattern pieces at the yoke shoulder seam, matching the seamlines. This provides a complete neck curve for the next step.

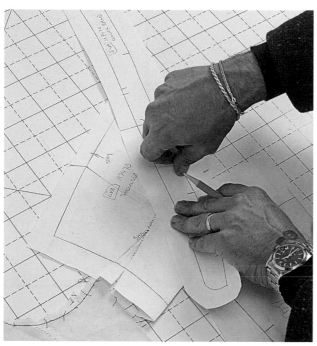

6. Walk the collar band seam along the neck seam, starting at the center front to the first seam (the front yoke seam). Mark the placement of that seam on the band. Then proceed to walk the collar band along the neck seam and mark the shoulder line placement on the band.

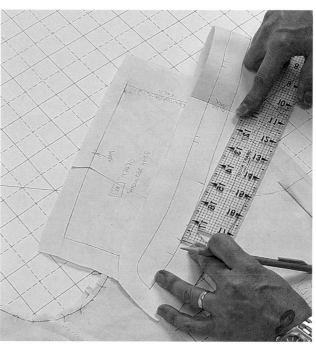

7. Note these two marks. This is the amount you need to remove from the collar band.

8. You need to alter the collar flap as well. Align the collar flap to the collar band from the center front and continue the new lines from the collar band up onto the flap.

9. Fold or cut out the alteration on the collar band and collar flap and tape the ends back together.

CORRECT THE PAPER PATTERN

VERTICAL SEAMS

1. Working down the muslin, pin the side-front panel onto the pattern, aligning the stitching lines.

2. Slip a piece of tracing carbon between the pattern and muslin, and use the tracing wheel to trace the princess-line corrections.

3. Next, trace the grid alteration in the upper chest area.

4. Reposition the carbon and trace the side-seam correction.

5. The pattern is marked and ready to alter. Make sure to go over all of the marked lines with a pencil to affix the marks.

CHEST FULLNESS

1. For the correction, I use the grid method (see pp. 51–53). Mark the center axis and gridlines on the double-ended dart. Extend these gridlines to the princess seam.

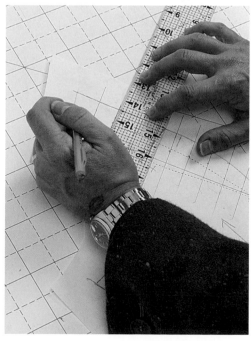

2. Measure the distance between the two lines of the dart and transfer that measurement along the grid to the closest princess seam.

CORRECT THE PAPER PATTERN

CHEST FULLNESS (CONTINUED)

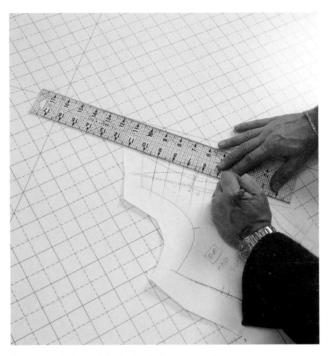

3. Connect the points to draft the new princess seam.

4. Measure and compare the original princess seam length to the new princess seam length to determine the difference.

5. Correct for the difference by lowering the shoulder end of the new princess seam so it measures the same as the original seam length.

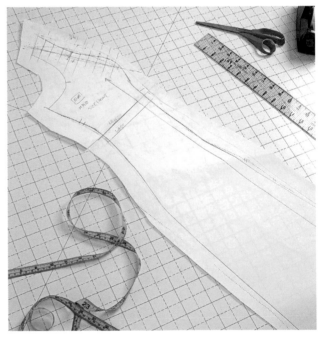

6. The finished side-front panel.

BACK

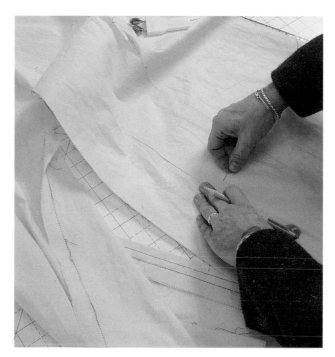

1. Pin the center-back muslin panel to the pattern.

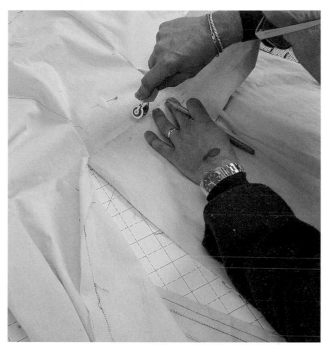

2. Trace the waist correction from the muslin to the pattern following the same method used previously.

3. Remove the pins, lift off the muslin, and reveal the correction.

4. Pin the side-back muslin panel to the pattern.

CORRECT THE PAPER PATTERN

BACK (CONTINUED)

5. Trace the side seam alteration.

6. Reposition the tracing carbon and trace the waist correction onto the pattern.

7. The side panel is marked and ready.

8. Measure the amount of alteration at the center back and note the measurement. This alteration is a no net change because the center-back alteration is folded out parallel to the original waist all the way across.

9. Extend this alteration across the center back and onto the side-back panel.

10. Fold out the parallel lines on the center-back panel and the side panel and tape them closed. True the seamlines on the side panel.

11. Extend the hem on both pieces by the amount you folded out at the waist. This brings the side seam measurement back to the original length.

NOTE: I call this a no net change alteration. Technically, it lifts the hip curves of the pattern so they match the curves on the body.

CORRECT THE PAPER PATTERN

SLEEVES

1. Measure the correction amount on the sleeve length. Mark this correction parallel to the length line on the sleeve pattern.

2. Fold out and tape closed the correction on the pattern. True the sleeve seams, and you're finished with the first fitting. Sew these changes into a new (or revised) muslin and take a second look at the fit.

TIP // AS I MENTIONED BEFORE, FOR STRAIGHT SHIRT SLEEVES, CORRECT THE LENGTH AT THE ADJUSTMENT LINE INDICATED ON THE PATTERN. IF YOU HAVE AN EXTREME CHANGE IN SLEEVE LENGTH (3 IN. OR MORE), SPLIT THIS CHANGE INTO TWO LOCATIONS—THE UPPER SLEEVE AND THE LOWER SLEEVE. THE RESULTING UNDERARM SEAM SHAPE WILL BE MORE PLEASING.

SECOND FITTING: MAKE REFINEMENTS

Evamarie's round-two alterations are minimal. They consist of smoothing the side seams at her hips to create a flattering line and adding some shape to her waist at the small of her back.

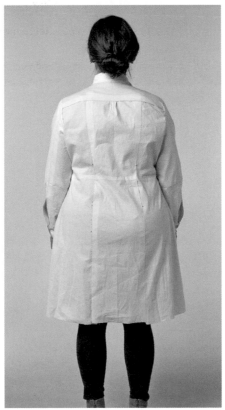

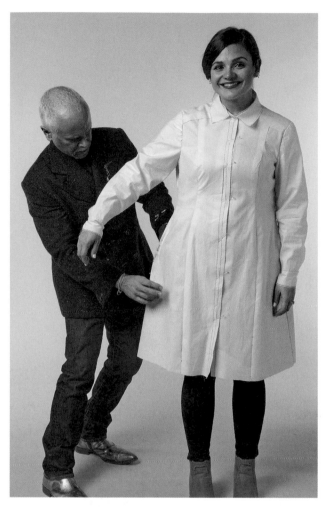 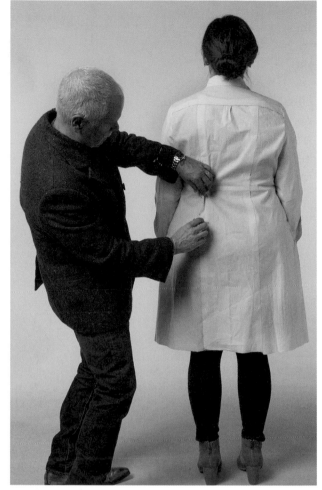

1. On the muslin, I've pinned out the alterations parallel to the seamlines. When pinning this way, mark along the pins instead of making hash marks. The perpendicular pins indicate where these alterations begin and end.

2. I added a little more shape at the waistline on the back by pinning out the princess lines slightly.

3. Since these alterations are minimal, I don't take the muslin apart, but simply mark the seamlines on the paper pattern and trace out the amounts that need to be adjusted.

FINAL FITTING

Compare Evamarie in this altered muslin dress to the photographs of the original muslin on pp. 120–121. This is a classic pattern Evamarie can wear for years as a dress or coat; she could even shorten it for a jacket.

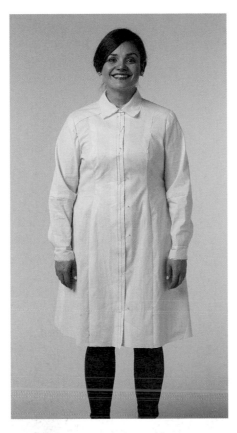

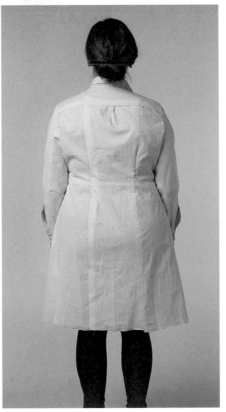

AFTERWORD: IT'S ALL ABOUT THE RESULTS

I HOPE YOU'VE ENJOYED READING THIS book and learned from my experience. But now I want you to see the result of all this work!

Compare the difference between the muslins before we started working and the final fitted muslins. I liken it to the difference between garments that look like an unmade bed and garments that enhance the figure and beauty of the wearer. Nothing makes you feel as good as wearing a garment that fits; look at the fun our *Threads* models are having!

Consider developing a small wardrobe of patterns—a good jacket, blouse, skirt, and coat, for example—that you can then make in many different fabrics, changing details with each new piece to customize them. With this wardrobe of patterns, you can concentrate on making the clothes you want to wear.

If there is a sewing group in your area, or an independent fabric store with a following of like-minded people who want to help each other with fitting, get involved! The added benefit you get is meeting new people along the way. But do invest the time to go through the fitting process. You can see in the photos how different the beginning muslins are from the finished ones!

CAROL

NORMA

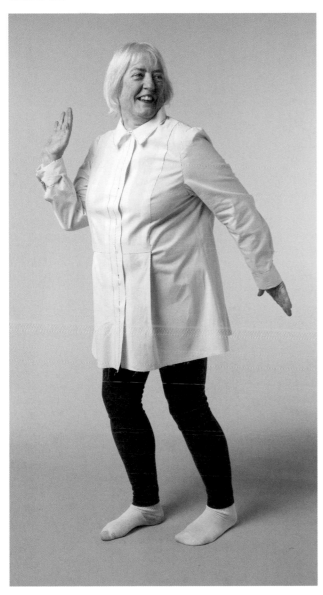

SARAH

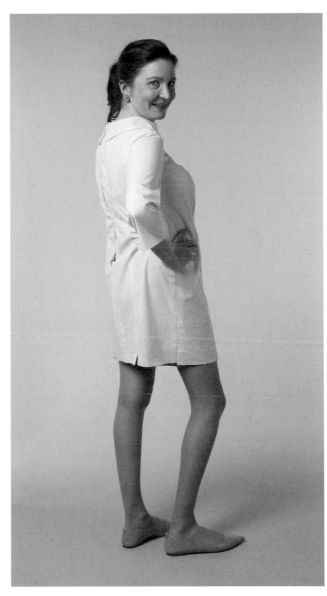

AFTERWORD: IT'S ALL ABOUT THE RESULTS

ROSANN

JEANNINE

EVAMARIE

APPENDIX 1: ESSENTIAL MEASURING POINTS

FRONT UPPER BODY AND BODICE

The bust is the primary source of bodice-fitting issues for most women. Note that most patterns are drafted for a B cup. If your cup size is larger, your measurements are likely to show insufficient width across the pattern front, and possibly insufficient length from shoulder to waist. You may need to make a full-bust adjustment.

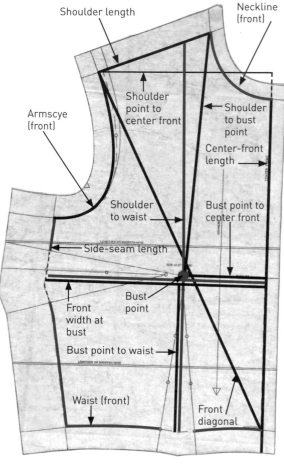

Shoulder length

Neckline (front)

Armscye (front)

Shoulder point to center front

Shoulder to bust point

Center-front length

Shoulder to waist

Bust point to center front

Side-seam length

Bust point

Front width at bust

Bust point to waist

Waist (front)

Front diagonal

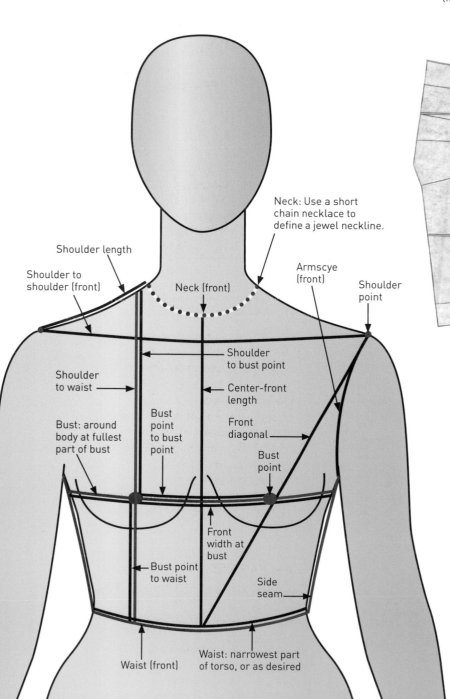

Shoulder length

Shoulder to shoulder (front)

Neck (front)

Neck: Use a short chain necklace to define a jewel neckline.

Armscye (front)

Shoulder point

Shoulder to bust point

Shoulder to waist

Center-front length

Bust point to bust point

Front diagonal

Bust: around body at fullest part of bust

Bust point

Front width at bust

Bust point to waist

Side seam

Waist (front)

Waist: narrowest part of torso, or as desired

TIP 1 //

Measure the body.
Establish reference points and lines on the body by applying ¼-in. adhesive dots (good for marking the bust and shoulder points), elastic bands (helpful for finding the waistline), narrow adhesive tape (draping tape or automotive masking tape), and even small ink dots on the skin. When taping horizontal lines, make sure they're parallel to the floor. Vertical lines should be perpendicular to the floor.

BACK UPPER BODY AND BODICE

Posture, musculature, and bone structure affect how garments fit the back. Many patterns are designed without much shaping in back, particularly in the shoulder and upper back. If you have forward or uneven shoulders, a rounded upper back, a swayback, or another idiosyncrasy, you may need to add darts or shaping to seams. These fit changes are best done on a muslin.

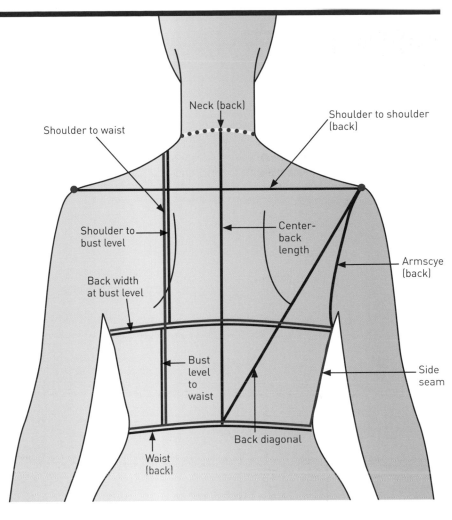

Neck (back)

Shoulder to shoulder (back)

Shoulder to waist

Shoulder to bust level

Center-back length

Back width at bust level

Armscye (back)

Bust level to waist

Side seam

Waist (back)

Back diagonal

Neckline (back)

Center-back length

Shoulder to bust point

Shoulder to waist

Armscye (back)

Back width at bust level

Bust level to waist

Back diagonal

Side-seam length

Waist (back)

TIP 2 //

Mark patterns. You'll need a ruler, tape measure, and pencil or marker to mark and measure the pattern tissue. Begin by drawing the seamlines on all the pattern pieces. Measure the seamlines between intersecting stitching lines, omitting the seam allowances and subtracting the dart intakes. Horizontal measurements should be perpendicular to the grainlines.

DIAGRAM KEY

———————— Mark and measure these points and lines.

– – – – – – Omit dart intake from the measurement.

——————— Measure only.

APPENDIX 1: ESSENTIAL MEASURING POINTS

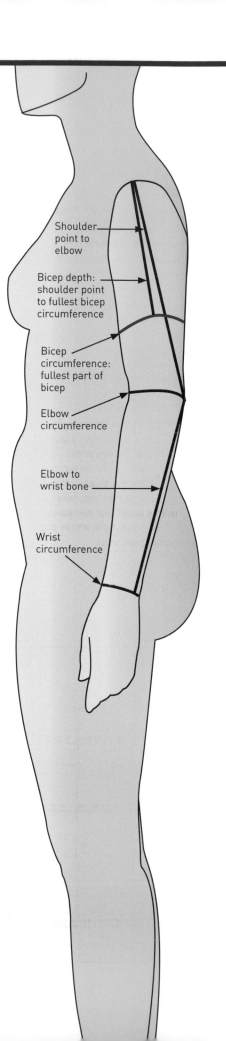

ARM AND SLEEVE

It's common for sleeves to fit poorly around the biceps. Tightness here is uncomfortable and can throw off the fit of the sleeve cap over the shoulder as well.

To find the bicep depth, mark the biceps at the fullest point and measure from the shoulder point to the marked line. Determine the arm lengths with the arm slightly bent. Measure from the shoulder point to the elbow and from the elbow to the wrist.

TIP 3 //

Compare dimensions. Remember that many pattern pieces represent one side of the body. Therefore, horizontal measurements across the torso must be divided by 2 when you're comparing them to the pattern tissue. To compare leg circumferences with a pant pattern, add the pant front and back measurements at the thigh and the knee.

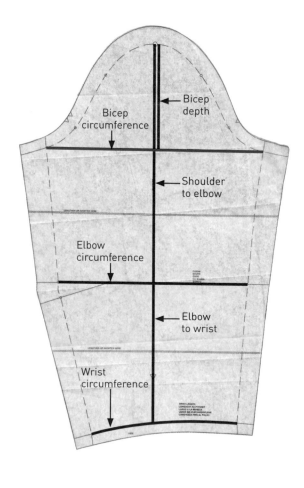

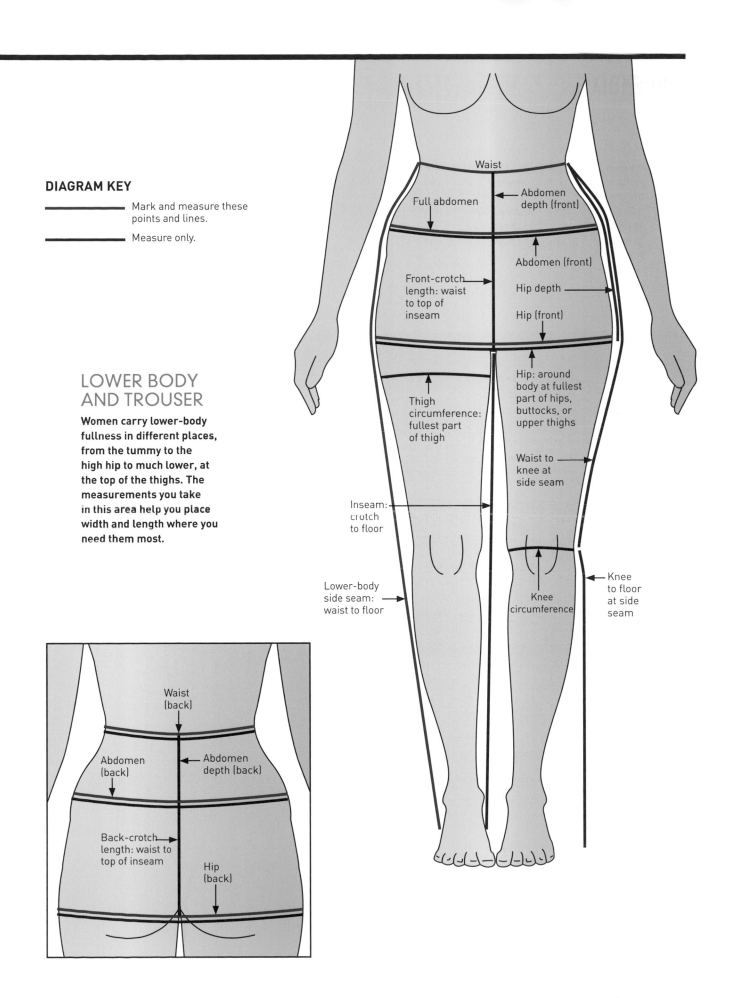

DIAGRAM KEY

—————— Mark and measure these points and lines.

══════ Measure only.

LOWER BODY AND TROUSER

Women carry lower-body fullness in different places, from the tummy to the high hip to much lower, at the top of the thighs. The measurements you take in this area help you place width and length where you need them most.

Waist

Full abdomen

Abdomen depth (front)

Abdomen (front)

Front-crotch length: waist to top of inseam

Hip depth

Hip (front)

Hip: around body at fullest part of hips, buttocks, or upper thighs

Thigh circumference: fullest part of thigh

Waist to knee at side seam

Inseam: crotch to floor

Lower-body side seam: waist to floor

Knee circumference

Knee to floor at side seam

Waist (back)

Abdomen (back)

Abdomen depth (back)

Back-crotch length: waist to top of inseam

Hip (back)

APPENDIX 2: WEARING AND DESIGN EASE

WHEN YOU'RE FITTING PATTERNS, COMPARING YOUR measurements to the pattern isn't enough. The pattern creator had added two different ease amounts to the measurements. First, a standard wearing ease is added to the measurements so you can move and be comfortable in the garment. Second, the style of the garment dictates extra design ease. You don't have to add ease to a commercial pattern—that's done for you.

The chart below lists standard wearing ease and design ease amounts for various garments and style preferences. Anything beyond standard ease amounts influences the style of the garment. Use this chart to provide information on how much more ease a very loose-fitting garment provides versus a close-fitting garment—not on how to fit a garment. To learn more about ease, go to www. threadsmagazine.com.

GARMENT	STANDARD WEARING EASE	DESIGN EASE				
		Close-Fitting	Fitted	Semi-Fitted	Loose-Fitting	Very Loose-Fitting
Dresses, Blouses	2-in. bust	0-in.–2-in. bust	3-in.–4-in. bust	4-in.–5-in. bust	5-in.–8-in. bust	over 8-in. bust
	1-in. waist					
	2-in. hips					
	1-in.–1½-in. armhole					
Jackets	4-in. bust		3-in.–4-in. bust	4-in.–5-in. bust	5-in.–10-in. bust	over 10-in. bust
	2-in. waist					
	4-in. hips					
	2-in.–3-in. armhole					
Coats	6-in. bust		5-in.–6-in. bust	6-in.–8-in. bust	8-in.–12-in. bust	over 12-in. bust
	3-in. waist					
	6-in. hips					
	3-in.–4½-in. armhole					
Skirts, Pants		0-in.–1-in. hips	2-in.–3-in. hips	3-in.–4-in. hips	4-in.–6-in. hips	over 6-in. hips

APPENDIX 3: FULL BUST ADJUSTMENT

THERE ARE TWO steps in adjusting a pattern for a full bust. One adjustment gives additional length to get the garment up and over a prominent bust. The other adjustment enlarges the front circumference. You can follow both steps or just one to fit your bust. Make bust adjustments after correcting the shoulder slope.

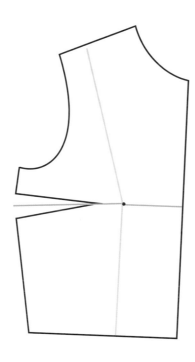

LENGTH

1. For the front length alterations, draw a line perpendicular to the center front, through the bust point and out through the side seam below the armhole, and through the existing dart if there is one. If there is no side dart, this adjustment will create one.

2. Compare the measurements on the pattern to the body or sloper. (See Appendix 1: Essential Measuring Points on pp. 222–225.)

3. Cut the pattern and spread along the horizontal cut to lengthen the front as needed.

CIRCUMFERENCE

1. Draw a line parallel with the center front from the waist, through the bust point, and out through the shoulder seam for front circumference alterations. To increase the circumference, cut the pattern along the vertical line. Spread the pattern, as shown below, to enlarge it to fit your measurements with ease added. Add paper into the openings and tape.

2. If the waist circumference isn't larger than the original pattern, you can taper the front into the side seams at the waist or hem to re-establish the original measurement.

APPENDIX 4: ROTATE A DART

DARTS COME IN DIFFERENT STYLES depending on the placement and garment style, but all darts go through two stages: the patternmaking dart and the dressmakers' dart. This is how they differ.

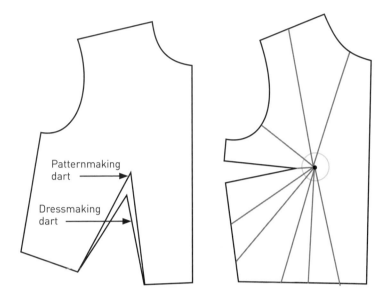

Patternmaking dart

Dressmaking dart

PATTERNMAKING DART

This dart goes all the way to the apex (or bust point). When a dart is moved on the pattern, the changed pattern needs to remain flat. Using a patternmaking dart keeps everything flat.

To create a patternmaking dart, extend the legs of the bodice dart to the apex.

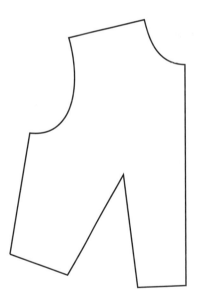

DRESSMAKING DART

This is the final dart sewn into a garment. It is drafted after making the patternmaking dart. The point is centered between the patternmaking dart's legs and is generally 1½ in. before the bust point. Note: If you sew the dart all the way to the apex, you get a cone-shaped bust. (This is not a good look.)

Remember these three rules:

- Dart legs should be the same length.
- Dart points are always a minimum of 1 in. to 1½ in. from the bust point. (For a fuller bust, 2 in. to 3 in.)
- Draft all darts to the bust point. When the rotation is complete, shorten them from the bust point by 1 in. to 1½ in.

1. Use a compass to draw a circle (blue) with a 1-in. to 1½-in. radius around the bust point.

2. Draw a line where you want the new dart from any outside edge or seam to the bust point (examples drawn in pink). Draw a line from the center of the existing dart through the bust point.

3. Cut along the original dart legs, abut them, and tape the dart closed to the bust point.

4. Cut along the new dart line to the bust point. The pattern will flatten, and the new dart will open along the line you cut. It is the right size to replace the original dart.

5. Tape paper into the new dart and true the seamlines. Shorten the dart length to touch the circle. Taper the bodice length into the side seam.

APPENDIX 5: THREE-STEP SLEEVE

WHEN MAKING PATTERN adjustments, the sleeves suffer, even if you've carefully selected your fabric and a pattern that is a simple design. Even after just a few standard adjustments, the sleeves aren't right, and you wonder where you went wrong.

In the examples here, the models' arms look almost identical, but hardly any patterns are made that will fit this arm, for two reasons: first, because the pattern is drafted with the front and back armhole the same curve size and shape; and second, because the front armhole should be at least ½ in. shorter with a greater curve. These issues show up on both the bodice and sleeve patterns.

THE BODY

Notice the arms on these models. They are different lengths and circumferences and even different shapes, but they all have one common characteristic—the arms all bend naturally forward from the elbow.

Look at the shape of the upper arm at the shoulder; on most of the arms, you will see the ball joint of the arm located on the front of the shoulder. It appears that on only one person (Evamarie, shown in the bottom right photo) the ball joint is located on the top of the shoulder near the shoulder seam location.

THE PATTERN

Compare an average sleeve and armhole pattern (outlined in black in the top drawing on p. 230) to what is calculated from the body. For this drawing, I'm using a sloper to show

the difference (the pink line). This explains why the sleeve has trouble fitting.

The human back is generally 2 in. longer and 2 in. wider than the front. Most bodice patterns are cut with the back and front armholes close to the same size and shape. The same is true of the sleeve pattern. Many sleeves are straight and typically do

not follow the shape of the arm. The front and the back of the sleeve cap seam are basically the same shape on a pattern for an arm and shoulder that are shaped differently and move in different directions.

APPENDIX 5: THREE-STEP SLEEVE

Here are some tips to combat the problems in fitting your sleeve. Follow the steps in order to get the right results.

1. Fit the bodice and the armhole first. Get the shoulder slope correct and make sure the armscye fits the arm. Consider lifting the underarm seam for a more comfortable sleeve.

2. Make sure the sleeve has adequate circumference, and mark the muslin with a grainline going from the sleeve hem to the shoulder matching point. This point does not have to match the one on the bodice, but it does have to be on the grain.

3. Mark the bicep perpendicular to the grainline.

4. If the sleeve is straight, consider adding an elbow dart. Also consider fitting the muslin above the elbow to avoid the arm bending the sleeve and making wrinkles.

5. Pin the sleeve to the bodice while the bodice is being worn. There are two ways to get good results:

A. Pin the grainline to the bodice with everything else free so you can make sure the sleeve falls with the grainline perpendicular to the floor. Then pin each side to be certain the bicep stays square to the grainline and parallel to the floor. Continue pinning between pins to evenly attach the sleeve to the armscye. This method removes fit differences from under the arm.

-OR-

B. Align the underarm seams and sew the sleeve to the bodice under the arm between the notches. Try on the garment with the sleeve and ease the grainline straight up and pin it to the shoulder. (In both examples, the grainline does not have to meet the match point, but it does have to be plumb.) Smooth the sleeve up and out and place a pin midpoint between the first pin and a notch on both the front and back of the sleeve. Continue pinning between pins to evenly distribute the ease and correct the shape of the sleeve cap. This method pins out any excess sleeve cap length or shape differences along the sleeve cap seam.

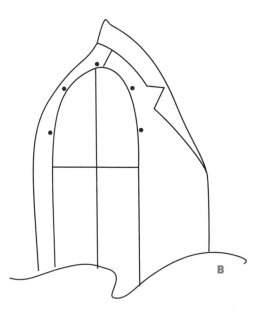

INDEX

INDEX

INDEX

Side seams
  altering, 24, 37, 49, 80, 87, 91,
    99–101, 109, 111, 118, 123
  correcting for distortion, 157
  correcting the paper pattern, 169,
    185, 186, 200–201, 208, 212,
    213
  marking the muslin, 132, 150,
    162, 195, 203
  pinning out wrinkles related to,
    99–101
  second fitting alterations, 173,
    192, 215–16
  setting the corrections, 132, 150,
    162, 195
  shaping, 20
  straight, 24, 79
  truing, 143
Skirts
  flared, fitting a, 125
  smoothing out, 109
  straight, 39
Sleeve cap, 190
Sleeves
  correcting the pattern, 135, 171,
    187–90, 201, 214
  cuffs (see Cuffs)
  fitting, considerations and tips for,
    229–30
  length of, 16, 64
  measuring points, 224
  pinning out wrinkles related to,
    81–82, 92, 102, 112, 118, 126
  second fitting alterations, 192
  setting the corrections, 131, 149,
    175, 194, 204
  sewing muslin, 70
Smart Fitting alteration method
  distortion, correcting for, 56
  net gain, 40, 48
    with a grid, 51–53
    slash-and-spread method,
      48–50
  net loss, 40, 42
    with a grid, 44–47

at a seam, 42–43
smoothing out skirts, 109
no net change, 40, 54–56, 91
principles of, 40–41
Staystitching, 69, 70, 71

T
Tools and materials, 58–59

U
Upper-body circumference, 86

V
Vertical seams
  altering, 21, 22, 94, 97, 108, 122,
    125
  correcting the pattern, 208–9
  pinning out wrinkles related to, 80
  See also Princess seam

W
Waist
  correcting the pattern, 155,
    165–66
  fitting issues related to placement
    of, 33
  measuring points, 225
  pinning out wrinkles related to,
    79, 87, 92, 108–11, 118, 123,
    125
  second fitting alterations, 192,
    215–16
  setting the corrections, 151, 162,
    204
Wearing ease, 6–7, 80, 88, 146, 226
Wrinkles
  identifying in the first fitting,
    74–75, 84–85, 94–95,
    104–5, 114–15, 120–21
  mobility versus appearance,
    balancing, 88

net gain, that indicate the need for
  a, 48
net loss, that indicate the need for
  a, 42
no net change, that indicate the
  need for a, 54
pinning out (see Pinning out
  wrinkles)
reading, 5, 73
shark fin, 89

Y
Yoke
  correcting the pattern, 197–99,
    205–7
  fit adjustments made through
    altering, 19, 24, 29, 31, 32, 35
  setting the corrections, 195–96,
    204

Z
Zippers, 71